Piano-Playing Revisited

Eastman Studies in Music

Ralph P. Locke, Senior Editor
Eastman School of Music

Additional Titles of Interest

Piano-Playing Revisited

What Modern Players Can Learn from Period Instruments

David Breitman

UNIVERSITY OF ROCHESTER PRESS

The University of Rochester Press gratefully acknowledges generous support from the Martin Picker Fund of the American Musicological Society, supported in part by the National Endowment for the Humanities and the Andrew W. Mellon Foundation.

First published 2021

University of Rochester Press
668 Mt. Hope Avenue, Rochester, NY 14620, USA
www.urpress.com
and Boydell & Brewer Limited
PO Box 9, Woodbridge, Suffolk IP12 3DF, UK
www.boydellandbrewer.com

ISBN-13: 978-1-64825-010-1
ISSN: 1071-9989 ; v. 176

Library of Congress Control Number: 2020952163

This publication is printed on acid-free paper.

Printed in the United States of America.

Dedicated to the memory of my musical partner and spiritual brother, Sanford Sylvan (1953–2019)

Contents

List of Illustrations

Figures

Examples

Unless otherwise indicated, the newly set musical examples follow the text of the first editions.

Preface

I have subtitled this book "*What* Modern Players Can Learn from Period Instruments," but I'd like to begin by addressing *Why*.

A Personal Odyssey

My interest in historical keyboards began while I was a piano student in Boston in the 1970s. Boston was then (and still is) a center for early music, a magnet for specialist performers and ensembles. I had a series of transformative lessons with the harpsichordist Robert Hill immediately after his studies with Gustav Leonhardt in Amsterdam; the near-fanatical attention that he brought to articulation made an indelible impression on me. Not long afterwards, my first encounter with a fortepiano produced a eureka moment: I had been struggling with Beethoven's G minor cello sonata and realized that my problems with its brilliant passagework, which drowns out the cello unless played *mp* instead of *ff* as Beethoven indicates, would be solved by such an instrument. More than a decade passed, but I eventually made my way to Cornell University and spent three wonderful years as a doctoral student of Malcolm Bilson; with his help I acquired a fortepiano of my own, and performed that very cello sonata—playing *ff* to my heart's content without drowning out my cellist.

I continued to perform on modern as well as historical instruments, and began teaching at Oberlin Conservatory, working with both "modern" students and Historical Performance majors. As a teacher and as a performer, I became increasingly interested in applying what I had learned from old instruments to "regular" performance. Two unexpected opportunities gave me the chance to do just that. The first was a novelty concert called *Aha! Concerto* at the Carmel Bach Festival in 2008. I was to perform the Rondo movement of Beethoven's C major concerto, beginning at the fortepiano, and then, after a dramatic interruption by the emcee, switching to a modern concert grand. I agreed, although not without apprehension. I feared that the fortepiano would seem like a historical curiosity—the audience thankful and relieved as it was carried off the stage—rather than a serious instrument in its own right. I needn't have worried. Some listeners preferred the sound of the modern piano, but everyone could appreciate the trade-off between the clarity and intimacy of the early instrument versus the power and warmth of the modern one. I was glad to have done it, despite the challenge of playing two radically different pianos in rapid succession in public.

The second experience was completely unplanned. I was preparing to perform the two Mendelssohn cello sonatas with my Oberlin colleague Catharina Meints. The dress rehearsal went well: my copy of an 1819 Graf piano and her gut-strung Amati sounded wonderful together, and we were looking forward to the evening's concert. Less than an hour before the concert was to start, an air-conditioning malfunction caused the humidity in the hall to plummet drastically, making it impossible to stabilize the tuning of the fortepiano. We either had to cancel, or use the sturdy, iron-framed Steinway instead. The audience was expecting Mendelssohn "on original instruments," and so were we. But, as I explained from the stage, we cared about the music more than our instruments and we were up for the challenge. Adrenaline pumping, we adjusted to the radically different piano. We played very differently from how we had rehearsed—but not in the "normal" way, either. Some listeners thought that the house Steinway sounded quite unusual that night: no wonder, since I spent the evening coaxing Graf sounds out of it. We enjoyed ourselves enormously, and so did the audience. At the time I would have been hard pressed to explain exactly what I did, and I haven't stopped thinking about it.

Because of those experiences I now use two very different pedagogies. The first one reflects the way I studied the fortepiano at Cornell, as a completely independent instrument. Oberlin's undergraduate piano majors can take secondary fortepiano lessons with me just as they might elect secondary instruction in voice or another instrument. To minimize confusion or potential conflict between our lessons and their work at the modern piano, I insist that students work on pieces they haven't played before, and that they practice them only on the fortepiano. Although conceptually clean, this strategy lacks an explicit bridge between our work at the fortepiano and its potential application to the modern piano.

The second, more elaborate approach involves the direct comparison of historical and modern instruments. I first tried this out during my 2009–10 sabbatical year, in a seminar at the Université de Montréal entitled "Period Instruments as Tools for Today's Pianists." The idea was to remove the fortepiano from the early music arena, proposing it simply as a vehicle to help pianists play better. The course was divided into four workshops, and included master's and doctoral students. Jean Saulnier, head of the piano department, oversaw the entire project and co-taught the first segment.[1] We began with a restored 1848 Pleyel—the least unfamiliar of the instruments—for our exploration of Chopin, moving to a copy of an 1819 Graf for Schubert and late Beethoven, and to a ca. 1800 Walter (the maker of Mozart's piano) for Haydn, Mozart, and early Beethoven. The final workshop, devoted to Bach and the clavichord, was quite different from the others, because the challenges of this radically different instrument led us to focus on keyboard technique as much as style.

Over the course of the semester, the students found new strategies for making music on the unfamiliar instruments. Much of what they needed was already in their scores: dynamic indications, pedal markings, slurs, and accents that had previously seemed puzzling or irrelevant now appeared perfectly suited to the instrument in front of them. Whether they enjoyed playing the old instruments or not, all felt that the music would never look the same again. Their insightful comments convinced me that this book needed to be written, and some of their words have made it into these pages.

The Scope of this Book

We continue to study and perform old pieces, attending conscientiously to every detail, because we love them and are moved by them. But they are products of a particular time and place, and a visit with their composer would surely reveal more than what is captured in the scores. Fortunately, twenty-first-century musicians have access to the past in ways that were unimaginable until recently: autograph manuscripts can be consulted online, historical treatises have been republished, translated, indexed, and compared, and period instruments have been restored, copied, and recorded. For some, those instruments are just museum pieces and the idea of playing one in public elicits only bemusement or sympathy. But they can be powerful tools for making sense of old scores and historical treatises and they have certainly helped *me* become a better musician. What they teach can be used at any piano; this book will show you how.

It is a practical book, not a theoretical or speculative one. The emphasis is on the music: how it sounds on period instruments, why the notation looks as it does, and how we might use those insights to enrich performances at a modern piano. Readers searching for a technological history of the piano, or for discussion of eighteenth- or nineteenth-century theories of aesthetics, will have to look elsewhere. Neither is it a polemic: I only draw on treatises and other historical sources for advice and for context, not for justification. If I manage to make a score more understandable, or to open new avenues for interpretation, then I will have succeeded.

The book is far from comprehensive. Instead, it focuses on the music I care about most deeply and the problems I have found most perplexing. It's framed by two philosophical chapters: the first one situates today's musicians and their repertoire in a historical context, while the last explores the impact of the Historical Performance approach on an individual's creativity. The second chapter, entitled "With Broad Strokes . . .," summarizes the lessons I've learned, organized by musical topics such as the relationship between melody and accompaniment, or the use of the pedal. The central chapters consider the pianos and piano music of Haydn and Mozart, Beethoven, Schubert, and Chopin, and are followed by a chapter devoted to the clavichord. Each is filled with musical examples that illustrate how composers' notation reflects the characteristics of historical keyboards, and how that recognition can help performers on any instrument.

I hope this book provides some ideas and techniques you can use. But I also hope some of you will be inspired to seek these instruments out and play them for yourselves, so that you can draw your own conclusions. This is getting easier all the time as more old pianos are being restored and increasing numbers of high-quality replicas are being produced. I'm especially gratified to see these instruments at music schools, where they can be consulted like books in the library. We study music history, since it would be unthinkable not to know the basic facts about the composers whose music we play, and also music theory, without which it's impossible to understand the language in which the pieces are written. Hands-on experience with historical instruments is equally indispensable—our only window into the physical reality, both tactile and auditory, of the musical past.

Note to the Reader

Pitch names in the text use the following system: CC C c c^1 c^2 c^3, where c^1 is middle C.

A suite of videos available on the book's product page (https://boydellandbrewer. com/piano-playing-revisited-hb.html) complements the text, including demonstrations of the moderator pedal, of the clavichord action, and of representative musical examples from the text.

Acknowledgments

Without Malcolm Bilson's tireless, decades-long campaign for the fortepiano, a book like this one would never have been written, let alone read. For thirty-five years he has been an inspiration to me—as a teacher, performer, scholar, and friend: this work is for Malcolm, a small token of my gratitude.

Directly after completing my DMA at Cornell, I began teaching at Oberlin, and Oberlin has been my productive academic home ever since. Thanks to Tom Kelly, Conrad Cummings, Jocelyn Swigger, Andrea McAlister, and Steven Plank for reading early versions of the manuscript; to Peter Takacs for our regular dissections of problems in Beethoven; and to countless others with whom I've had fruitful conversations over the years. But I'm grateful to my students above all, because, in the end, the book is about what I've learned from *them*. Some, notably Max Fleischman and Daniel Walden, will recognize their fingerprints on many of these pages; I can't thank them enough. Thanks also to Oberlin College's Grants office and to Pam Snyder personally for generous institutional support of this project—with a special shout-out to my student assistant Liam Kaplan for the elegantly typeset musical examples.

The book could not have been written without the assistance of my wife Kathryn Stuart, who has been by my side through this whole journey, and whose patience, encouragement, sage advice and careful proofreading have made it possible.

Chapter One

Music Making
Then and Now

Pianos Then and Now: Variety and Standardization

Despite the rapid pace of technological change over the past century, the piano as we know it—a pinnacle of engineering at the end of the nineteenth century—has barely altered since then. For the first two centuries of the piano's existence, however, change was the norm. The earliest pianos weighed little more than a harpsichord, about a hundred pounds; a modern concert grand weighs nearly a thousand. They grew steadily in range— from four octaves to more than seven—and in string tension, to produce ever more powerful sounds. The "harpsichord with soft and loud" (in Italian *gravicembalo col piano e forte*," hence pianoforte or fortepiano— piano for short) created by Bartolomeo Cristofori in Florence around 1700 was a delicate instrument, suitable for solo playing or for accompanying a singer (rather like a lute); today's piano can compete with a symphony orchestra.

The basic nature of piano tone changed too. Classical-period instruments produced transparent sounds with a sharp attack and a quick decay; their clear articulation favored a "speaking" style of playing. Later ones had a longer-lasting singing tone, better suited to Romantic music. There was also great variety in their design, as hundreds of small workshops responded to ever-changing musical tastes with creativity and ingenuity.

But at the turn of the twentieth century, the piano industry consolidated and focused instead on the large-scale production of standardized instruments imitating the successful Steinway model.[1] The new uniformity would have surprised musicians of the past. Franz Liszt personally endorsed various pianos with very different designs while Chopin reportedly preferred an Erard piano when he felt "out of sorts" and a Pleyel when he felt "in good form";[2] Today the Steinway type is still ubiquitous; its only challengers come from two opposing directions: a flood of innovation in the electronic arena, and the small-scale production of replica fortepianos.

Thanks to recordings, more and more music-lovers have heard those forte-pianos. Malcolm Bilson's set of the complete Mozart concertos from the 1980s was a watershed; since then, other adventurous players have explored an ever-widening range of repertoire using a variety of historical instruments, both antiques and replicas. Nevertheless, most pianists have never played anything but a Steinway-type piano, and the terminology we use reflects this reality. We have a special word—*fortepiano*—to refer to the older types of piano. *Pianos* (i.e., the Steinway model) are played by *pianists*, while other keyboards such as the harpsichord, clavichord, and fortepiano are reserved for specialists.

The historical situation was precisely the reverse. *Clavier* was the normal German word for a keyboard instrument in the eighteenth century, and it could refer interchangeably to a harpsichord, clavichord, or piano ("*Hammer-klavier*" = keyboard with hammers); a professional keyboard player such as Bach or Mozart would have been expected to be at home with any keyboard instrument, including the organ.

The Clavichord

Every piano, from Cristofori's first model to the modern Steinway, pro-duces sound in the same way: a hammer is thrown against the strings and its velocity determines the loudness of the sound. The organ, harpsichord, and clavichord operate on completely different principles, and of these three, only the clavichord shares the piano's ability to vary the strength of the sound by means of the touch. Since its sensitive action demands a great deal of control from the player, C. P. E. Bach maintained that a good clavichord player will play the harpsichord well, but that the reverse was not necessarily true.[3] For the same reason, I imagine that the earliest pianists, including Haydn and Mozart, adapted to the new instrument by drawing on their experience at the clavichord, rather than the harpsichord. The clavichord still has valuable lessons to offer today's pianists, so it has its own chapter in this book.

Different Approaches to Music of the Past

Pianists of today are engaged in a remarkable project: keeping alive a musical repertoire that represents a multitude of styles and spans more than three centuries. But not so long ago, most musicians played in only one style—that of their own contemporary music. And during the eighteenth and nineteenth centuries, that style changed rapidly. While instrument builders responded to the demands of the latest music, composers took advantage of the possibilities offered by the new instruments. Older music, along with earlier instruments and performing styles, quickly seemed passé or even primitive. Like today's moviegoers, musical audiences were eager for the latest works, although a nostalgic taste for selected older ones might linger—as long as they were not *too* old. The *Concerts of Antient* [*sic*] *Music* series that operated in London from 1776 to 1848 typifies this attitude. According to their policy, "Antient" meant anything more than twenty years old, and they felt free to modernize the scoring of the pieces they played. In the same spirit, Schumann, an avid admirer of J. S. Bach, composed piano accompaniments for Bach's solo violin and cello pieces to make them more accessible to his contemporaries, just as remakes of old movies do today.

By the end of the nineteenth century, this paradigm was changing. The reigning musical style was Romanticism, and the newest piano was the Steinway, essentially in the form we know it today. A historical canon was taking shape, and concerts were filled with more and more old music. Some works were updated through transcriptions and arrangements (e.g., Busoni's of Bach, Liszt's of Schubert), while new "interpretive" editions adapted older repertory to Romantic taste and the capabilities of the new pianos. Example 1.1 shows an excerpt from one such edition, while Example 1.2 reflects the notation of Mozart's autograph score. The 1893 version[4] replaces four short articulations with a single, long slur and introduces a crescendo fork that imposes a continuous shape on Mozart's independent motives. The "romanticizing" editors were neither ignorant nor foolish: they were simply updating old music to suit current tastes and instruments, just as Schumann had done. For them, in the final decades of the nineteenth century, Wagner's *Parsifal* was contemporary music, and the Steinway piano was state-of-the-art. "Endless melody" was Wagner's goal, so Mozart was fitted out with longer lines, all the better to show off the sustaining power of the new pianos. And Steinway, winning all the prizes at international exhibitions, was imitated by every piano maker who hoped to stay in business.

Example 1.1. Mozart, Sonata in F major, K. 332, mvt. 1, mm. 1–4 (Schirmer edition, 1893).

Example 1.2. Mozart, Sonata in F major, K. 332, mvt. 1, mm. 1–4 (slurs following the autograph).

Tastes change, and after the First World War, Romanticism fell out of fashion. Not just in music: Figures 1.1 and 1.2 show the rejection of decoration and the primacy of form in early twentieth-century architecture. Osborne House (Figure 1.1), a nineteenth-century Italianate building, is replete with asymmetrical decorative elements; the modernist Bauhaus building (Figure 1.2) offers nothing but flat surfaces and right angles. Similarly, the neo-classicism of Stravinsky or Copland demanded rigor, not sensuality, and the same performance aesthetic was now applied to older repertoire. Musicologists and publishers joined forces to produce new editions of the standard works, from Bach and Scarlatti through Schumann and Chopin, in which the Romantic overlay of nineteenth-century editors was removed. They called them *Urtexts*, meaning "original text," and one of the tenets of musical modernism was obedience to that version. The result—in print and eventually in performance—was a kind of "objective" rendering whose kinship with the architecture of the Bauhaus was evident in every streamlined, unsentimental gesture.

But the apparent sterility of eighteenth-century musical scores reflects an economical mode of notation, not the composers' desire for uninflected performances. Evidence from treatises and descriptions of music-making suggest

Figure 1.1. Osborne House, Isle of Wight, built between 1845 and 1851. Photo created between ca. 1890 and ca. 1900. Courtesy of the Library of Congress Prints and Photographs Division, Photochrom print collection.

a richly expressive style, where the subtlety expected of performers was rarely notated or else was communicated through symbols such as slurs, time-signatures, and barlines that no longer convey all of their original implications. Without a corresponding re-evaluation of musical training, the adoption of the new editions often led to lifeless, unsatisfying performances, since players were reluctant to introduce anything—such as variety in dynamics, touch, or tempo—not explicitly indicated by the composer. Or they were misled by indications that produce markedly different effects on modern instruments than on those with which the composers were familiar.

That re-evaluation of musical training did come, in the form of the early music movement, and it was counter-cultural and controversial. The comments of the prominent violinist and conductor Pinchas Zukerman, quoted in the *Toronto Globe and Mail* (March 2000), were typical: "The first time I heard that shit, I couldn't believe it. It's complete rubbish, and the people who play it. . . . Maybe one or two or a half-dozen have wonderful musical minds. But I certainly don't want to hear them perform."[5] No one is likely to voice that sentiment in public any more, but another unfortunate outcome

Figure 1.2. Bauhaus Building by Walter Gropius, 1925–26, photo Willmington-Lu, Yakob Israel, 2018.

has taken its place: many musicians (including major symphony orchestras) have simply stopped performing baroque and early classical music, leaving that repertoire to the specialists.

As a result, today we have two distinct approaches to music of the past. The first, which I call the Traditional Approach, continues the practices of the late nineteenth century, seeking to apply a unified set of instruments and techniques to the widest possible repertory. Even the clothing we still see on our symphonic stages—tailcoats and white ties—marks the origins of this style. The second approach, introduced by the early music movement, and now usually known as Historical Performance (since it doesn't apply exclusively to early music), proceeds from the opposite assumption. As Nikolaus Harnoncourt, the famous conductor, cellist, and early music pioneer argued, "each period has precisely the instrumentarium best suited to its own music."[6] With the performance techniques described in treatises from Mozart's time, the original slurring shown in Example 1.2 creates a longer line through the accumulation of shorter, articulated units—a style perfectly matched to the quick decay of the eighteenth-century fortepiano.

Appreciating different musical styles for their own sake is a characteristically modern idea. Today's musical landscape features specialist ensembles devoted to specific repertories: baroque orchestras, renaissance vocal ensembles, contemporary music groups, alongside specialized instrumentalists like baroque violinists and flutists, harpsichordists, fortepianists, and clavichordists. What's missing is a middle ground, where pianists who still want to play a wide range of repertoire on a modern piano can take advantage of insights from specialist performers and current musicology.

How can we do that? Historical Performance is sometimes referred to as HIP (Historically Informed Performance) but I propose that we think instead about Historically Informed *Preparation*. It shares the clever acronym, and reminds us that what's in the performer's mind is far more important than what sort of instrument is on the stage. By taking old instruments into account as we prepare, we discover what the composers took for granted. Think of the move between historical and modern pianos as a kind of transcription. An experienced pianist preparing to play the reduction of an orchestral score knows the value of listening to the original. Similarly, in the words of one of the seminar students, "it's much easier to produce a correct interpretation of a given work when you can use the composer's own creative tool to discover his intentions." Although I'm uncomfortable with the notion of a "correct interpretation," a sincere effort to understand a composer's intentions provides a solid foundation, regardless of the choices a performer ultimately makes.

A performance is not a history lesson, and the insights from period instruments can't always be applied directly to the modern piano. But historical specialists can be valuable allies, and old instruments offer a fresh view of the score, opening your ears and eyes to new sounds and new ideas. No one has a monopoly on any of the repertory, and, as we'll see, the composers themselves were anything but rigid about their choice of instruments.

Chapter Two

With Broad Strokes . . . (An Overview)

I like to say that music prior to 1800 *speaks*, while subsequent music *paints*. The former must be *understood*, since anything that is spoken presupposes understanding. The latter affects us by means of moods which need not be understood, because they should be *felt*.[1]

—Nikolaus Harnoncourt

The modern piano is especially good at painting, while the older instruments, especially those from before 1800, excel at speaking. The modern one evokes strong feelings with long melodic lines and grand dynamic contrasts; early pianos focus the ear on details like the beginnings and endings of sounds, the spaces between them, and the precise calibration of emphasis—the very same attributes that make speech understandable and compelling.[2]

This attention to detail makes the older instruments demanding taskmasters. They require focus on the *micro* level: the dynamic shape of an ornament, the exact length of individual notes, or the careful articulation of a series of short slurs. I often say, "the good thing about the fortepiano is that you can hear everything; the bad thing is that you can hear everything!" At the modern piano, it's tempting to adopt a big-picture view and favor the principal voice, overlooking nuances of dynamics and articulation as well as details in the accompanying parts.

Cultivating a "speaking" style can counterbalance habits developed in response to the modern piano and the Romantic repertoire. Harnoncourt draws a line at 1800, but I see a more gradual transition, with plenty of "speaking" in Beethoven and even in Chopin, although the qualities of "painting" gradually predominate. Ultimately, this meticulous work is beneficial for performance on *any* instrument, and is applicable to a wide range of repertoire.

Learning from Old Instruments

Playing an instrument is a two-way street. We ask things of our instruments, and they respond—but not always in the way we expect. Their effect on us is immediate, and they begin teaching us the moment we touch them. The old instruments have a lot to offer, and while some of their lessons are immediately apparent, others come only with long and patient study. Here, in broad strokes, are the observations that will be fleshed out with specific musical examples in subsequent chapters. (Some of the features listed here are demonstrated on the website, https://boydellandbrewer.com/piano-playing-revisited-hb.html.)

- They have limits, both in compass and in dynamic range. Pieces written for Mozart's small piano with its 61-note range can seem strangely diminutive and conservative when transferred to the 88-note Steinway; returned to his instrument the music reappears life-sized and innovative.
- Their smaller dynamic range creates greater intimacy. Chopin's Pleyel excelled in the salon; the solos in Mozart's concertos are qualitatively different from the *tuttis*, conceived so that the piano never has to compete with the sound of the full orchestra.
- Each sound has a sharper attack and a quicker decay than its counterpart on the modern piano. (This difference is most pronounced on the earliest instruments: Chopin's Pleyel sustains much longer than Mozart's Walter, though not nearly as long as a Steinway.) This makes it more difficult to sustain a long line, especially at a slow tempo, but it promotes the articulation of small details.
- The touch is lighter and shallower, making it much easier to control small-scale articulation.
- They promote polyphony. The modern piano encourages the player to bring out one melodic line, keeping the rest of the texture in the background; the older instruments easily project several equal voices.
- They are much less uniform across their range than a modern piano. Modern instruments of all kinds (and modern vocal technique) are designed for homogeneity of color from the bottom to the top of the range. Older wind instruments had a more noticeable register break; violins had more variation in color from string to string, and pianos had distinctive registers. On an older piano, repeating a theme at a different pitch level produces a stronger contrast in timbre and character than on a modern piano.

- They require less pedal. On the modern piano, the difference between "pedal on" and "pedal off" is very great; unlike the older instruments, our pianos sound quite dry when played without pedal. At least two different factors are at work here:

  ❧ The modern piano's dampers are large and heavy. They need to be, to effectively damp the tremendous power of the instrument, just as a sports car that can reach 150 mph must have correspondingly big brakes to bring it to a stop. The comparatively light dampers of older instruments leave a certain amount of resonance behind, even when playing without pedal. This effect is especially characteristic of English pianos, whose gentle damping surrounds the tones with a generous "after-ring."

  ❧ Every musical tone is composed of the fundamental frequency of the note plus a mixture of overtones. The modern piano's basic sound favors the fundamental, but depressing the pedal adds more overtones because the higher strings can vibrate sympathetically. On the early piano sympathetic vibration is less necessary, because its basic sound is bright and very rich in overtones[3] (like a harpsichord) and also less effective, because its smaller range offers fewer sympathetic strings.

Bear in mind that there is no such thing as "the fortepiano." Besides the developments that took place over time, the two main piano-building schools—English and Viennese—represented quite different aesthetics. While early Viennese fortepianos epitomized the "speaking style," English instruments always featured a more *cantabile*, singing sound. (French pianos are closer to the English tradition: Chopin called Broadwood the "English Pleyel.") Much of this book focuses on Viennese-style pianos and the music of Viennese composers. But in the history of piano making, English pianos play a significant role—both the modern piano's action and its tonal ideal have more in common with the English tradition than the Viennese.

Learning from Treatises

The eighteenth century was known as the Age of Enlightenment, when scholars tried to organize all available knowledge and present it systematically. Comprehensive treatises were published on a wide variety of subjects, and music was no exception. For our purposes the most important books are C. P.

E. Bach's *Essay on the True Art of Keyboard Playing*, Johann Joachim Quantz's *On Playing the Flute*, Leopold Mozart's *A Treatise on the Fundamentals of Violin Playing*, and Daniel Türk's *School of Clavier Playing*. Alfred Einstein, in his preface to the Mozart book, says this about Quantz and Bach: "Both go far beyond the boundaries of mere 'Tutors' of their instruments; they are guides to the whole musical *style* of the time."[4] It can indeed be hard to separate the two since many aspects of style depend directly on the physical properties of the instruments themselves.

What follows is only a brief overview; for a much fuller discussion of the historical materials with generous quotations from a wide range of sources—including ones not translated elsewhere—the indispensable resource is Sandra Rosenblum's *Performance Practices in Classic Piano Music*.

Articulation

Articulation plays a crucial role in eighteenth-century style, and writers devoted considerable attention to slurs, dots, and strokes (also known as *wedges* or *daggers*).

Slurs have three properties:

1. legato connection between the notes;
2. stress at the beginning (Leopold Mozart says diminuendo throughout the slur, no matter how many notes there are);
3. early release of the last note, to separate the slurred group from what follows.

In certain cases, there is also a fourth: the notes may be held down for the length of the slur ("overholding" or "finger-pedal"). C. P. E. Bach and Türk give examples where the slur covers an arpeggiated pattern; Bach explains this as equivalent to "French notation,"[5] in which each note is written as a separate voice and given its full length. Türk gives a fuller explanation, illustrated in Example 2.1.

When there is a curved line over harmonies which are to be slowly arpeggiated, as in the following examples, it is customary, especially in compositions of agreeable character, and the like, to let the fingers remain on the keys until the appearance of the next harmony. For this reason the following measures *(a)* can be played as shown in *(b)*.[6]

Example 2.1. Türk, *Klavierschule*, p. 345.

Dots and strokes indicate detached notes, or *staccato*. The confusion between these two signs is captured perfectly by Türk: "The detaching or separating of tones is indicated as we know by a stroke or a dot above or below the notes. . . . The signs [dot and stroke] have the same meaning, but some would like to indicate by the stroke that a shorter staccato be played than that indicated by the dot."[7] C. P. E. Bach also believes that the stroke and dot are interchangeable. For the practice pieces published as part of his treatise (*Probestücke*) he provides fingering on every note, and explains that he will use dots to indicate staccato to avoid confusion between the stroke and the numeral "1."

The "some" who maintained that the stroke is shorter include Louis Adam, author of the Paris Conservatoire's official method from 1804,[8] and Francesco Pollini,[9] a composer most famous for his *Metodo per Clavicembalo*. Where Mozart (whom Pollini knew) and Beethoven stood on this is not clear, their manuscripts containing signs that range from a clear dot through a long, emphatic stroke (Example 2.2 shows this range in Beethoven's handwriting). I find this variability very expressive and believe performers should be free to interpret the marks on a case by case basis, but editors of this music face a serious dilemma. Older Henle editions opted for only dots; Schenker, in his edition of the Beethoven sonatas for Universal (republished by Dover) used only strokes; other recent editions including the newest ones from Henle try to distinguish between them, with mixed success.

As for notes without slurs or dots, the treatises agree that—at least until the early nineteenth century—these were held for less than their notated length unless the composer explicitly marked them *tenuto*, or *ten*. Writers did disagree, however, about the exact length of these notes. Türk criticized C. P. E. Bach's rule to hold them for half their value; he recommended three-quarters, confirming a trend which led to the recognition of legato as the default touch by the 1820s. For rapid, unslurred passagework, eighteenth-century writers prescribe this "normal" or "ordinary" touch, which on a Viennese fortepiano results in an unforced, mild *non-legato*. At the modern piano, where a quick *non-legato* can sound labored, it is tempting to ignore the distinction and play all figuration legato whether or not there are slurs.

Example 2.2. Beethoven, Sonata for Piano and Violin in C minor, op. 30, no. 2, mvt. 2, m. 33 (autograph manuscript, Beethoven-Haus, Bonn).

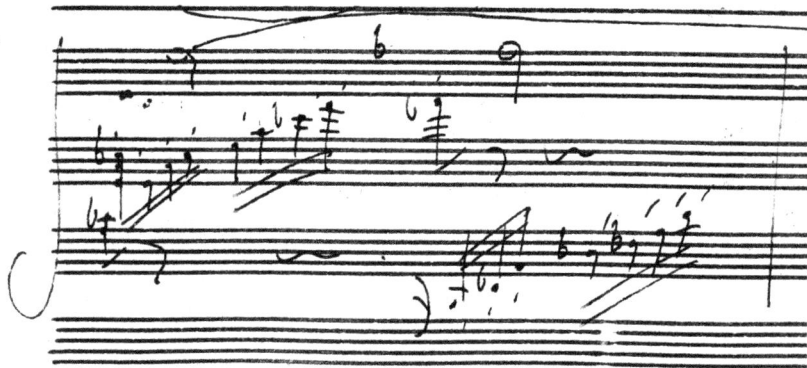

Dynamics

Dynamics were frequently compared to light and shade, and players were expected to use them, even in the absence of indications: According to Leopold Mozart, "one must know how to change from *piano* to *forte* without directions and of one's own accord, each at the right time; for this means, in the well-known phraseology of the painters, Light and Shade."[10] Small-scale variations would have been especially important on the clavichord, with its relatively narrow dynamic range. Carl Friedrich Cramer reports: "All who have heard [C. P. E.] Bach playing the clavichord must have been struck by the continual refinement of shadow and light which he throws over his performance."[11]

Musical dynamics were also related to language. Harnoncourt's comparison of eighteenth-century music to speech is historically justified: theorists like Türk also used this analogy, and it would have had even more resonance for his readers because rhetoric, the classical art of constructing and delivering speeches, was still part of their school curriculum.

> Whoever would read a poem and the like in such a way that it becomes comprehensible to the listener must place a marked emphasis on certain words or syllables. The very same resource is also at the disposal of the practicing musician. The question which then arises is: What tones are to receive a special emphasis?[12]

The answer is determined by the musical context. Here are the primary factors:

Meter: strong beats are louder. Leopold Mozart:

> Generally the accent of the expression or the stress of tone falls on the ruling or strong beat, which the Italians call Nota Buona. . . . These may be called the strong beats on which the chief stress of the tone always falls if the composer has indicated no other expression.[13]

Harmony: dissonances are louder. Quantz:

> To excite the different passions the dissonances must be struck more strongly than the consonances. Consonances make the spirit peaceful and tranquil; dissonances, on the other hand, disturb it . . . The more, then, that a dissonance is distinguished and set off from the other notes in playing, the more it affects the ear. But the more displeasing the disturbance of our pleasure, the more agreeable the ensuing pleasure seems to us. Thus the harsher the dissonance, the more pleasing is its resolution.[14]

Note values: long notes are louder, as Leopold Mozart shows in Example 2.3:

> It is customary always to accent minims [half notes] strongly when mixed with short notes, and to relax the tone again.[15]

Example 2.3. L. Mozart, *Treatise*, p. 219.

Note that all of these comments refer primarily to the expressive fluctuations within motives and phrases, not the large-scale dynamic plan of a piece.

Rhythm

Today's musicians pride themselves on absolute rhythmic accuracy and can use electronic devices to develop it; the eighteenth-century attitude to rhythm and its notation was rather different. French writers described an effect called *inégalité* (inequality) where certain notes that looked equal on the page were to be played unequally, like a swung rhythm in jazz. Quantz suggests that this applied more broadly. In the section of his treatise "On Good Execution in General in Singing and Playing" he says:

the quickest notes in every piece of *moderate tempo*, or even in the *Adagio*, though they seem to have the same value, must be played a little unequally, so that the stressed notes of each figure, namely the first, third, fifth, and seventh, are held slightly longer than the passing, namely the second, fourth, sixth, and eighth, although this lengthening must not be as much as if the notes were dotted.[16]

As for actual dotted notes, the modern insistence on a precise 3:1 relationship between a dotted note and the following short one is not supported in the sources. Both overdotting (holding the long note longer and making the short note quicker) and its opposite, underdotting, are prescribed by the sources in various contexts. The most common case of underdotting involves synchronizing the short note with the last of a triplet in another voice, as suggested by the alignment shown in Example 2.4, published under Bach's direction.

But the presence of a conflicting rhythm is not the only context for shortening or lengthening a dot. Leopold Mozart recommends overdotting as a general rule: "There are certain passages in slow pieces where the dot must be held rather longer than the rule demands if performance is not to sound too sleepy. . . . The dot should in fact be held at all times somewhat longer than its value."[17] Although "at all times" may be an exaggeration, Mozart is not alone in this opinion. Türk says: "It is customary, for the most part, to dwell on dotted notes longer (and therefore to play the following shorter notes more quickly) than the notation indicates."[18] This can be done on any instrument, of course, but the heightened contrast between stressed and unstressed notes—a result that sounds natural on early pianos—may require extra care at the modern piano to avoid caricature.

Example 2.4. J. S. Bach, Partita no. 1 in B-flat major, BWV 825, Corrente, mm. 1–2 (original edition, Leipzig, 1731).

The Impact of a Historical Approach

By drawing on treatises and direct experience with old instruments, the historical approach blends theory and practice. And since some aspects of playing were never fully documented, it is especially gratifying when the instrument itself clarifies something in the written sources, or the reverse. Virtually every parameter of performance is affected, as will be outlined here.

Tempo Choice

Many factors influence tempo, above all the performer's view of the *Affekt* (emotional content) of a piece. But the instrument, like the acoustical space, also plays a role. Every experienced performer has encountered the relationship between tempo and acoustics. A wet acoustic limits how fast one can play without losing intelligibility; a slow tempo that sounds majestic in a resonant room can become deadly dull in a dry one. For similar reasons, the modern piano's long-sustaining tone permits—even encourages—slow tempi that are unrealistic on a fortepiano with its quicker decay. But a slow tempo that prioritizes the beauty of the modern piano's sound may lessen the impact of the harmony or phrase structure, as will be shown in later chapters.

Dynamics

The modern piano makes much more sound than its predecessors, although this is not obvious on recordings since the volume is controlled by the listener. With nearly limitless power at their command, modern pianists can structure the dynamics of a piece in a linear way. The loudest sounds are reserved for the climax; quieter sections lead gradually to louder ones by means of carefully graded crescendos. The dynamics thus operate at what might be called the *macro* level; many pieces might be schematized as one big crescendo, or a large-scale crescendo–diminuendo. Of course, this is an oversimplification. Most performances also include direct contrasts between soft and loud on a smaller scale, and, especially in a longer piece, the crescendo–diminuendo shape will be applied to individual sections of the work.

At a historical piano, where the absolute dynamic range is more limited, other strategies need to be employed. When playing Chopin we may want a long shape that gradually builds intensity, and on a modern piano it's possible to do this directly, just by getting steadily louder. Because early pianos "run out of gas" sooner, a series of successively stronger waves may be more effective than a straight climb. This approach fits the evidence we have concerning Chopin's own playing: he used *forte* only occasionally, and was known for extreme refinement in the lower dynamic levels. According to his student Karol Mikuli, he detested loud piano playing, calling it "the sound of a dog barking."[19] By using the smaller shapes—at any piano—we create a more detailed design that is more engaging for the listener.

Meter and Accent

Without accentuation, musical performance would be lifeless and unintelligible. Only when notes are differentiated from each other by varying levels of emphasis can we perceive shapes, phrases, and ideas. Depending on the style and the individual composer, a score may contain many explicit directions for accentuation, or it may contain few or even none.

Theorists of the eighteenth century distinguished between two kinds of accents: *rhetorical* (sometimes called *pathetic*) and *grammatical*. *Rhetorical* accents are the ones we would call *expressive*; they are often indicated by signs (>, ^, ', <>, *sf*, *rf*, *fp*, *f*). *Grammatical* accents derive from the meter and phrase structure; they are determined by rules that eighteenth-century musicians were expected to know, and are normally not notated.[20] Since classical composers expected performers to project the meter by means of these accents, they could work against that structure for expressive purposes. (The opening of Mozart's Sonata in G, K. 283, discussed in the next chapter, is an excellent example.) And while these intricate patterns of accentuation create variety and musical interest, players of the modern piano experience an opposing pull—a sort of sonic momentum that favors equality and a smooth surface, the familiar image of passagework as a string of (perfectly matched) pearls. This quest for evenness still leaves room for expressive accents, but the grammatical ones are often underplayed or even deliberately avoided.

On the older instruments, that pull is not so strong. The modern piano's large mass of sound, like the inertia of a large truck or boat, resists sudden changes of speed or direction. A fortepiano, in contrast, behaves more like a sports car whose quick responses inspire its driver to accelerate aggressively, turn sharply, and stop abruptly. Strong shaping of a melodic line with prominent contours and sudden accents is easier at the fortepiano, because the louder sounds dissipate quickly. That's why an accentuation scheme may not transfer directly from a historical instrument to a modern one: an approach that sounds convincing on the fortepiano may seem exaggerated, or even brutal, on a modern piano. Different styles of accent may have to be

Example 2.5. Beethoven, Sonata no. 12 in A-flat major, op. 26, mvt. 1, mm. 1–8.

employed. At the fortepiano, a *quantitative* or *percussive* accent—where the note is simply played more forcefully—is often the most effective; to create a comparable effect on a modern piano, the pianist may need to use subtler *agogic* techniques, such as lengthening or delaying ("placing") the note.

Small- vs. Large-scale Structure

Consider the first movement of Beethoven's op. 26, a set of variations on a theme thirty-two measures long (the opening is shown in Example 2.5). With the big picture in mind, one might try to construct a single shape out of the entire theme, making each variation a block in the overall structure. But since the tones of the early piano do not sustain as long as those of a modern piano, it is difficult—if not impossible—to create a smooth surface that spans an arch of that length. The alternative is to build a coherent structure out of smaller units. By organizing the first four measures around the dissonances in measures 2 and 4, the relative stability of the half-cadence in measure 4 can then be acknowledged with a breath before beginning measure 5.

These features can be brought out at any instrument, of course, but the modern piano allows us to step back and "paint" the entire phrase with a continuous, uniform tone. Without the generous resonance that enables this style of playing, the fortepiano player *must* depend on the details of inflection and articulation to sustain the musical line.

Beethoven's detailed dynamics (*cresc–sf–>–p* in mm. 3–4; *p–cresc–p* in mm. 7–8) and short slurs (especially the separation between m. 6 and m. 7) are certainly more comfortable at the fortepiano than at the modern piano, where they can seem fussy and even clumsy. But instead of treating them with embarrassment and reluctance, and minimizing them in the interest of

WITH BROAD STROKES . . . (AN OVERVIEW) ᴥ 19

Example 2.6. Beethoven, Sonata no. 3 in C major, op. 2, no. 3, mvt. 1, mm. 27–33.

a longer line, we can try to make them meaningful. Perhaps they represent an elaborate seduction with calculated approaches and retreats—or an imagined one, oscillating neurotically between confidence and timidity . . .

A highly nuanced performance may seem to focus the listener's attention on local events at the risk of obscuring the large-scale form. But it can also illuminate the big picture: clear distinctions between dissonances and consonances reinforce the harmonic structure, and emphasizing the first notes of slurred groups can bring out underlying melodic motions, as in Example 2.6 (note the descending line D–C♯–C–B–B♭–A–G–F).

Register

The distinct registers of early instruments reveal aspects of a composition that may be less obvious on the modern piano with its more consistent timbre. A player who is alert to these effects can employ different strategies to bring these out; particularly striking examples will be discussed in the Mozart, Schubert, and Clavichord chapters.

Texture and Counterpoint

At the modern piano, careful voicing (the differentiation of notes sounded simultaneously, making some louder than others) is an important attribute of high-quality playing. Experienced players strongly emphasize the principal part, while keeping subsidiary voices and accompanimental figures in the background. The modern piano generally sounds best when played this way; insufficient attention to voicing produces a drab, colorless sound. The opposite is true of earlier pianos: without the contribution of all the voices, the sound is thin. After working with historical instruments, students often come to appreciate details that had previously been hidden in the background. Reintroducing these elements at the modern piano requires precise balancing of the parts, but can lead to a more refined performance.

Two-Voice Textures: An Aside

The two-voice texture of much eighteenth-century music—vibrant and full on a harpsichord or fortepiano—often produces a dry, empty effect on the modern piano. Why should that be?

One explanation is *context*: we are accustomed to the full resonance of Romantic piano music, and simple two-part writing sounds old-fashioned—like an old black-and-white television show viewed on a big, high-definition screen. The same music played on a fortepiano sounds better because we don't have another context—we've never heard any other sort of music on the fortepiano.

But there is also an acoustical explanation. Since each of the fortepiano's registers has its own color, the two voices acquire distinct tonal characters. And *every* register of the fortepiano is rich in overtones compared to the modern piano, adding complexity as well as variety. (This is displayed graphically in the Appendix.) A single tone on a modern piano could be compared to the 8' flute stop on an organ, which has a relatively uncomplicated sound on its own. The rich sound that we associate with the full organ comes from the combination of pipes supplying the natural harmonics (overtones) of the fundamental tone, including the octave above the note being played, the twelfth above, and two octaves above. Mixture stops add a collection of even higher harmonics for additional brilliance. In other words, a simple two-part texture played on the overtone-rich fortepiano—or the organ—presents the ear with a much fuller spectrum of sound than the same texture on a modern piano.

As pianos changed, piano music also changed. To compensate for the flatter sound of individual tones, composers used chords, arpeggios, and octave doublings to add resonance. Increasing use of the pedal also brought the sympathetic vibration of other strings into play.

What can we learn from this? First of all, it gives us a truer picture of composers and their works. The two-part textures of Scarlatti or early Haydn were not the product of primitive compositional technique, but idiomatic responses to the instruments they wrote for. And with that perspective we can find ways to compensate for the characteristics of *our* instruments, maximizing the impact of the composers' original designs.

Pedaling

Many pianists are simply unaware of their use of the sustaining pedal. Typically, the pedal is kept depressed (ask a pianist to play a single chord, and the pedal will probably go down too), with frequent changes to maintain legato while avoiding harmonic clashes. This technique, known as *syncopated* or *legato* pedaling, consists in lifting the pedal at the arrival of a new bass or harmony (typically at the beginning of a measure or beat), and then depressing it shortly after. It's called *syncopated* because the pedaling is offset from the corresponding harmonies, and *legato* because it produces a seamless connection between tones.

The opposite approach—*rhythmic* pedaling—although infrequently used by pianists today, is virtually the only one prescribed by composers of the nineteenth century. Occasionally notated by Beethoven, and extensively by Chopin, Liszt, and others, it involves depressing the pedal simultaneously with the bass on the strong beat (indicated with the "Ped." symbol), and releasing it *before* the next harmony (indicated with the "*" symbol). Early pianos respond well to this approach, but the modern piano dissuades us from using rhythmic pedaling for several reasons:

- The difference in timbre between the pedaled and unpedaled notes is greater on the modern piano; we want to avoid the noticeable dryness that rhythmic pedaling introduces between changes.
- Each bass note rings much longer on the modern piano. We resist cutting it off by releasing the pedal; instead we try to connect it to the next one.
- The modern piano speaks relatively slowly. The initial attack of the hammer produces some unwanted noise, while the full, round tone of the note blooms slightly later. Syncopated pedaling prevents the noise component from being captured in the pedal resonance; the pedal only catches the new bass note once it is in "full bloom." The older piano's tone speaks more quickly and begins to decay much sooner, so the opposite incentive applies. We want to pedal earlier, to catch as much resonance as possible.

Syncopated pedaling may have been more common in the nineteenth century than the scores suggest: Carl Czerny described it in his *Vollständige theoretisch-practische Pianoforte-Schule*, op. 500, published in 1842,[21] Clementi asks for it in a few of his late compositions, and proposals were made for new ways to notate it. It certainly shouldn't be excluded in this repertoire, but rhythmic pedaling, rarely used by today's players even when explicitly called for by the composer, needs to be recognized and reinstated in the pianist's toolbox.

There are two other important differences between historical and modern use of the pedal:

- the possibility of a "normal" style of playing without any pedal at all;
- the option of keeping the pedal down for longer than we ordinarily think appropriate.

The implications of these factors will be explored in depth in the Beethoven and Chopin chapters.

Touch (the Length of Individual Notes)

The modern piano's resonant tone combined with a near-constant use of the damper pedal lends itself to legato playing, so legato has become the "default touch." At the fortepiano, with its shallow key dip and quick damping, the articulate quality of "ordinary" (non-legato) touch is clearly perceptible, and the precise length of the note compared to the surrounding space can be controlled for expressive purposes. As Türk states: "If the character of a composition is serious, tender, sad, etc., then the detached tones must not be as short as they would be in pieces of a lively, humorous, and the like, nature."[22]

Reimagining *non-legato* as the "default touch" for eighteenth-century keyboard music can lead to greater variety and a wider expressive palette, but be careful not to confuse the comfortable "ordinary touch" with an energetic staccato!

Articulation (Separating Groups of Notes)

The same factors that facilitate non-legato touch at the fortepiano also encourage subtle spaces between short groups of notes. The modern piano has a narrower margin for error: if the spaces are too large, the passage will sound choppy; if too small, the difference will be undetectable.

A Word about Creativity

It's easy for a pianist to become inhibited by the desire to "do it right." The score already specifies which notes to play, when to play them, and much more. It may seem that the Historical Approach gives the performer even less room for personal expression by proposing yet more rules, but I believe the opposite. A deeper understanding of how musicians of the past performed and notated their compositions can give us the confidence to express ourselves more fully (more about this in the Epilogue).

Chapter Three

The Early Days of the Piano: Haydn and Mozart

From Multiple, Interchangeable Keyboards to the Piano

When C. P. E. Bach published his *Essay on the True Art of Playing Keyboard Instruments* in 1753, the piano merited little attention. Although Cristofori had built his first one more than fifty years earlier, here's what the authoritative Bach thought a player needed to know about it:

> Of the many kinds [of keyboard instrument], some of which remain little known because of defects, others because they are not yet in general use, there are two which have been most widely acclaimed, the harpsichord and the clavichord. . . . The more recent pianoforte, when it is sturdy and well built, has many fine qualities, although its touch must be carefully worked out, a task which is not without difficulties.[1]

He then offers the following advice:

> Every good keyboardist should own a good harpsichord and a good clavichord to enable him to play all things interchangeably. A good clavichordist makes an accomplished harpsichordist, but not the reverse. The clavichord is needed for the study of good performance, and the harpsichord to develop proper finger strength.[2]

This was precisely the situation in the Mozart home when Wolfgang and his sister Nannerl, also a talented keyboard player, were growing up in the 1760s. The family owned a five-octave, two-manual harpsichord by Friederici and a five-octave clavichord; a small travel clavichord by Stein was acquired for the extensive tours of 1763–66.[3] Eventually, the piano became Wolfgang's primary instrument. In a letter from 1777, his mother wrote from Mannheim to her husband at home in Salzburg: "Indeed [Wolfgang] plays quite differently from how he used to in Salzburg, for there are pianos here, on which he plays so extraordinarily well that people say they have never heard anything like it . . ."[4]

Two years earlier, in 1775, an anonymous reviewer was less impressed:

> In Munich last winter I heard two of the greatest clavier players, Herr Mozart and Captain von Beecke; my host, Herr Albert . . . has an excellent fortepiano in his house . . . Mozart's playing had great weight, and he read at sight everything that was put before him. But no more than that: Beecke surpasses him by a long way. Winged agility, grace [and] melting sweetness [characterized his playing].[5]

Mozart's playing style must have developed dramatically ("he plays quite differently from how he used to") as he experimented with the new instrument; these experiments may also explain the surprising frequency of dynamic markings in the earliest piano sonatas, K. 279–284.

As for Haydn, he was a middle-aged, successful composer who had already written much of his keyboard music by the time the fortepiano became popular. But he too changed his style in response to the new instrument, as we can see from this letter to his student Marianne von Genzinger, from 1790:

> Your Grace will no doubt have received the new Clavier Sonata [Hob. XVI:49] by now ... It's only a pity that Your Grace doesn't own a fortepiano by Schanz, since everything is better expressed on it. . . . Your Grace might give your Flügl, which is still quite good, to Fräulein Peperl and buy yourself a new fortepiano . . . I know I ought to have composed this Sonata for your kind of Clavier, but I found this impossible because I am no longer accustomed to it.[6]

Evidently this sonata was conceived for the fortepiano, but when exactly did Haydn stop writing for the Flügl (harpsichord)? It would be useful to know which instrument he had in mind for each of his pieces, but the evidence is inconclusive. A group of Haydn specialists held a panel discussion on this topic in 1975; their consensus was that he began to write for the fortepiano around 1770, citing especially the extensive dynamic indications in the C minor sonata from 1771.[7] But other scholars continued to disagree. In 1979, Laszlo Somfai argued that "[s]onatas that appeared between 1780 and 1788 . . . were conceived in a *tentative fortepiano* idiom . . . [Only] the keyboard music of the years 1788–96 reflect a fully-fledged, mature crafts-manship of *fortepiano* writing . . ."[8]

Recognizing the impossibility of definitive answers, A. Peter Brown took a different approach in 1986. He proposed a "preferred instrument" for each of Haydn's keyboard pieces, along with an "other possible instrument" for many. He suggested the fortepiano as "possible" for pieces written as early as 1771, without arguing that Haydn had already abandoned the harpsi-chord at that point. The clavichord is listed as a "preferred instrument" for some pieces and as an "other possible instrument" for many more. Howard Pollack, in a 1991 article, places even more importance on the clavichord. In his view, "Haydn composed principally for the harpsichord from the 1750s to about 1765; the clavichord from 1765 to about 1780, and the fortepiano only sometime after 1780."[9]

A vignette by the English musician and historian Charles Burney sums up an attitude that may have been common in 1775, disparaging the harp-sichord while recognizing the natural progression from clavichord to fort-epiano. On a visit to Vienna, he heard an eight- or nine-year-old girl play the fortepiano extremely well and reported:

> I enquired of Signor Giorgio, an Italian, who attended her, upon what instru-ment she usually practised at home, and was answered, "on the Clavichord." This accounts for her expression, and convinces me, that children should learn upon that, or a Piano Forte, very early, and be obliged to give an expression to Lady Coventry's Minuet, or whatever is their first tune; otherwise, after long practice on a monotonous harpsichord, however useful for strengthening the hand; the case is hopeless.[10]

There were even more instruments. As C. P. E. Bach states, there were "many kinds" of keyboard instruments in the mid-eighteenth century: besides single- and double-manual harpsichords, clavichords, and pianos (grands and squares), there were *Tangentenflügel* (fortepianos with wooden jacks instead of hammers), and various combination instruments that held a harpsichord and an organ, a piano and an organ, or a harpsichord and a piano in a single case. Over the ensuing decades the piano gradually won out, but for most of this period we can assume that every keyboard compo-sition might have been played on a variety of instruments. This should be reassuring for us; if there was no "correct instrument" at the time, we needn't worry too much about playing the "wrong instrument" now. But we mustn't lose sight of the crucial fact that the modern piano is vastly different from *every* eighteenth-century instrument.

Even the narrow category of "late eighteenth-century five-octave Viennese piano" includes much more diversity than we find among today's instruments. A *Musical Yearbook* from 1796 describes the situation as follows:

> We have . . . two original instrument builders, Walter and Streicher, all the others imitate either the former or the latter . . . we can divide our greatest pianists into two groups as well. One of these groups . . . likes enormous noise . . . [and] for virtuosos of this kind we recommend Walter's kind [of piano]. The other group likes not only precise, but also sweet, melting playing. These cannot choose a better instrument than one of Streicher, or the so-called Stein model. [11]

Mozart is associated with both Stein and Walter. In a letter to his father from 1777, he wrote: "Späth's claviers had always been my favourites . . . But now I much prefer Stein's."[12] By 1785, Mozart had acquired an instrument by Walter, about which his father wrote to Nannerl, "Your brother's pianoforte has been taken at least twelve times from his house to the theatre or to some other house."[13]

At Oberlin we have two five-octave fortepiano replicas, a representative of each of these types. Unsurprisingly, conservatory students are initially more comfortable with the heavier, deeper touch of the Walter (the instrument for "virtuosos"); this model also seems to be the most frequent choice of today's replica builders (and their customers). But I have been pleased to watch my students learn to appreciate the Dulcken, a Stein-type instrument, as they become more accustomed to its sensitive, hair-trigger action. When compared with a modern piano, however, the differences between the two types are relatively minor.

After the unfamiliarity wears off, listeners and players are usually struck by the aptness of these instruments for the repertoire of the period. At the very first fortepiano recital I attended, I was seated next to a musicologist who remarked, after Malcolm Bilson's performance of a Haydn sonata, "at last, Haydn in clothes that fit!" I didn't recognize it at the time, but he was alluding to a letter in which Mozart writes to his father, "I like an aria to fit a singer as perfectly as a well-made suit of clothes."[14] Mozart seems to have had the same attitude towards instrumental composition. Unlike J. S. Bach, who freely adapted pieces from one medium to another, and whose keyboard pieces are generally suitable for harpsichord, clavichord or organ, Mozart's piano music seems tailor-made for the instrument he knew. As a young piano student, I thought that classical composers were conservative in their use of the instrument, since they never used the lowest or the highest notes and didn't enable the player to make an especially big noise. Only composers like Brahms, Bartók, or Prokofiev appeared to exploit the full resources of the piano. But seated at a seemingly delicate five-octave Walter, it becomes clear that Mozart made full use of *this* instrument's capabilities. His music fills up the fortepiano, just as Rachmaninoff or Ravel fill up the modern piano.

The Eighteenth-Century Viennese Piano: Elements of Performance

Range

Mozart's piano had a range of just sixty-one notes: five octaves FF–f³.[15] This is probably what a modern pianist notices first, along with the reversed colors of the keys (not true of all fortepianos, by the way). Many pieces written after about 1800 are unplayable on this instrument because they require notes above f³, but for the music that was designed for it, the restricted compass is extremely revealing. Example 3.1 is in B-flat major, so F—the dominant of the scale—is a very natural goal for the music, allowing Mozart to embrace both the lowest and highest notes of his piano. Strong crescendos leading to the high or low notes can bring this out directly and dramatically (notice that Mozart has reinforced both with octave doubling), but the modern piano's powerful bass may overstate the arrival at measure 118. An elegant diminuendo on the way down avoids that problem, but produces an entirely different impression from the one Mozart probably envisioned. On the softer fortepiano, a crescendo to the bottom is particularly effective, since that is the loudest part of the instrument.

Several techniques can be deployed in these contexts to produce a convincing, but not overpowering, crescendo at the modern piano: minimal pedal, a somewhat non-legato touch, a slight broadening of the tempo, and favoring the top note of the low octave. General advice for playing this music on a modern piano: never lose sight of the "goal posts" at each end of the five-octave instrument, and when a composer heads for one of them, make sure your arrival does it justice.

Register Effects

While the modern piano is designed to be as homogeneous as possible from bottom to top, minimizing register breaks, the individual sections of the

Example 3.1. Mozart, Sonata in B-flat major, K. 333, mvt. 1, mm. 8–9, 118–19.

five-octave piano have distinct colors and characters. The top octave sounds thin and silvery, quite different from the octave below it. The bottom octave can be snarly, with a sharp edge to it; the tenor is typically nasal and reedy. Although every instrument has its own colors, and individual listeners might perceive them differently, the variation in sound from register to register is unmistakable.

One student described his experience with this effect in the opening of Mozart's K. 533 shown in Example 3.2.

Example 3.2. Mozart, Sonata in F major, K. 533, mvt. 1, mm. 1–16.

In measure 8, the left hand repeats the melody that began the piece in the right hand. Even though the registers of the two are close together (they even share the same middle C), they speak differently. On the fortepiano, the right-hand version sounded quite like an oboe, with a distinctly reedy and trebly sound; the left-hand version was thicker and deeper, with a timbre that sounded more vocal than instrumental. I realized that what appeared on the page and at the Steinway to be a simple repetition could actually sound like an exchange between two instruments sharing the same melodic motive, but speaking with individual voices.

How might one give those voices their individuality at a modern piano? Taking a hint from the student's observations, we could play the right hand's "instrumental" version more evenly, then make the left hand more "vocal" with additional inflection for the interesting intervals a–g–bb–e.

In Example 3.3, the register shifts underline the structure. At measure 11, Mozart extends the initial phrase by repeating the material of measure 5 an octave lower. In the new register this figure acquires a darker, richer character until, two measures later, a wide leap brings us back to the "right" register and the "right" conclusion for the phrase. At the modern piano, it's easy to overlook these relatively small moves. But, once attuned to their significance, an attentive player can point them out through the deliberate use of timing, dynamics, or color.

Example 3.3. Mozart, Sonata in G major, K. 283, mvt. 1, mm. 1–16.

Texture

The distinct timbre of each register allows individual lines to be heard more clearly. Actively voicing one of the parts is largely unnecessary at the five-octave fortepiano—or at the harpsichord, where it is simply impossible—because each line has its own distinctive color. But at the modern piano with its relatively uniform timbre, it's up to the player to clarify the texture. The usual (and simplest) solution is to identify a "dominant" part, and to play it significantly louder than everything else. The resulting texture sounds clear, but only by giving up some of the complexity of the composition. K. 533 provides a good illustration of this as well, as noted by the student quoted above (refer to Example 3.2):

> When performing measures 9–14 on the Steinway, I favored the left hand [at m. 12], as it was a continuation of the melody, and relegated the right hand to a simple accompanying role by decreasing its dynamic. At the fortepiano, however, I discovered that natural voicing of the instrument easily allowed both voices to be heard without subordinating either. While the left-hand melody was rich, vocal, and lyrical, the right hand was more impish and playful, like yodeling.

Returning to the Steinway, he made sure to give the "yodeling" its due.

Even when the top voice is not very interesting, as in Example 3.4, the modern piano encourages us to bring it out, while overlooking—or at least underplaying—the other parts. At the fortepiano the two hands can be played with equal intensity, and the rhythmic energy of the quick notes contributes just as much to the overall impression as the upper line, without covering it. With careful balancing of the hands, the same effect can be conveyed on a modern piano.

Chords present an analogous situation. To avoid muddiness at the modern piano, one note (the top one if the chord is in the treble, the bottom if in

Example 3.4. Haydn, Sonata in F major, Hob. XVI:23, mvt. 1, mm. 44–46.

the bass) is normally voiced considerably louder than the others. This makes for greater clarity, but obscures a common feature of eighteenth-century keyboard composition: the use of texture to create *dynamic* contrast. This tactic—essential at the harpsichord—is still very effective on the fortepiano, where the power of a single note is limited, but a chord with all its notes struck equally sounds full and vibrant. On the modern piano, whose wide dynamic range makes this strategy unnecessary, it can still have its place, as in Example 3.5. The four-note chords on the second beats should be full and strong, despite—or because of—the *sfs* on the first beats. (More about this in the section "Music Not Written Specifically for the Piano," below.)

Example 3.5. Mozart, Sonata in F major, K. 332 mvt. 1, mm. 25–30.

The repeated chords at the beginning of the A minor Sonata K. 310 can sound clumsy and potentially overpowering, even on a fortepiano.[16] But minimizing them diminishes the drama of the piece: the accompaniment drives forward relentlessly for five bars, while the melody only advances one two-measure unit at a time. Subtly inflected and played with conviction, the chords can convey as much of the passion and despair of this passage as the melody does (Example 3.6).

Example 3.6. Mozart, Sonata in A minor, K. 310, mvt. 1, mm. 1–4.

Example 3.7 shows another kind of texture. At the modern piano, it is possible to treat the opening bars of K. 333 as a simple melody and accompaniment, playing the left hand especially delicately, so as not to cover the right hand's long notes. On the fortepiano, this strategy is scarcely viable: those dotted quarters don't sustain long enough, so the line dies on the second beat of every bar. If instead the level of the left hand is brought *up*, a dialog emerges between the two voices, with the left hand providing interest just as the right hand's long notes are fading away. Notice that the lower part is not simply an Alberti bass with interruptions, but an artfully designed complement to the right hand: rising against falling; triadic against scalar. The newly revealed polyphony adds life to the passage.

Example 3.7. Mozart, Sonata in B-flat major, K. 333, mvt. 1, mm 1–4.

To summarize: because of the fortepiano's transparency and the distinctive quality of its registers, each component of the texture can have relatively equal prominence and the parts balance themselves. The modern piano requires careful voicing. Without it the instrument sounds muddy, but overdoing it sacrifices rhythmic or contrapuntal interest.

Articulation

We can think about articulation in two ways. The first concerns the precise manner of attacking and releasing individual notes, which influences the music's character. The other focuses on whether adjacent notes are joined or separated from one another; this has implications both for expression and for syntax. It can also be a source of conflict or confusion because it's possible for notes that belong together *motivically* or *rhythmically* to be separated *acoustically.* This distinction will become important in the discussion of "successive slurs" and "slur+1," below.

Although articulation comes in infinite shades, only two symbols were used for its notation: the slur and the dot (three if we include the stroke[17]). These indications were rare in keyboard music written before ca. 1760, but Mozart's first published sonatas (from the 1770s) give directions for virtually every note, as do Haydn's late works. Did the increasing popularity of the piano create a new audience of amateur keyboard players who needed more guidance to interpret the music properly? Possibly, but I believe it's because the new, *galant* taste made these elements more important. With simplified harmonies and phrase structure but an emphasis on sentiment, this style demands an especially sophisticated delivery in which small details of articulation can carry a big expressive burden—just as they do in our everyday social interactions.

In spoken language, intelligibility depends on the clear articulation of consonants at the beginnings and endings of syllables. The manner of their delivery also dramatically affects the character of the message (try saying "Don't do that!" with varying degrees of emphasis on each of the consonants). Early pianos, with their sharp attack and quick damping, are especially well-suited to sensitive and varied "pronunciation." Of course, these same attributes make it more difficult to produce a sustained, singing line. Each instrument presents a different compromise among competing qualities; each has something to teach us.

Single Notes

Middle C played **mf** on my Steinway sustains for about four seconds (one measure of ¼ at M.M. = 60), then makes a diminuendo for another bar, and lingers on faintly for a third bar. On my Walter copy, the same note begins a sharp diminuendo almost immediately, is vanishingly weak in the second measure, and gone without a trace by the beginning of the third bar. The beginnings of the notes also differ. The Steinway's tones develop relatively slowly as the energy moves gradually from the strings, through the big bridges, and on through the heavy structure, producing a subtle crescendo. That big structure, once it begins vibrating, keeps the sound alive for a relatively long time. In the lightly constructed earlier pianos the sound propagates very quickly, and also dissipates quickly. Playing each of these instruments means adapting to these very different conditions. The advantages of the long sustain are obvious, and a modern piano that is deficient in this respect should probably be rejected by a potential buyer. But for the music of the classical era, it is often a disadvantage.

K. 309 (Example. 3.8) begins with a trumpet-like fanfare:

Example 3.8. Mozart, Sonata in C major, K. 309, mvt. 1, mm. 1–2.

When I sing this to myself, I use the syllables "Pahm, Pahm, Pahm-di-di-dee" (leaving out the initial grace notes). The consonant "P" guarantees a clear separation between C, G, and E (see the explanation in the box, p. 36), and that's how I play them on the fortepiano. On the modern piano, players typically connect these notes with the pedal, giving the impression of a slur over the entire motive. The articulated, unpedaled version sounds natural at the fortepiano because each note has its own rapid diminuendo, and the damper merely gives definition to the end of the sound, rather than actively interrupting it. The modern piano seems to discourage the articulated approach because the tones are still *developing* (i.e., getting louder) when it's time to cut them off. To create the effect heard at the fortepiano requires perfect control of the release of the key, using the damper to produce the diminuendo.

Example 3.9 features the repetition of a single note:

Example 3.9. Mozart, Fantasy in D minor, K. 397, mm. 20–22.

I sing this one as "paah-paah-paah-paah" with quite a bit of emphasis on every note. This articulation conveys insistence—fate knocking at the door, perhaps—but can sound very dry when played on the modern piano without pedal. With the pedal down, however, I hear something more like "baah-baah-baah-baah," or even "waah–waah–waah–waah." "Baah" minimizes the articulation (there is only a momentary interruption of sound as the lips close) while "waah-waah-waah" is essentially continuous, with the individual notes marked only by a change in the vowel (technically, a "glide" between "oo" and "ah"). In a sympathetic acoustic, slow releases of the key (without pedal) may produce the right balance between resonance and articulation; partial pedaling can also help achieve this effect.

In the field of phonetics, the term "articulation" refers to the specific actions of the tongue, lips, and throat by which speech is produced. The letter "P" is called a "plosive stop," and its articulation has three phases: first the "catch," in which the airway is closed by the lips, so no air escapes, then the "hold" in which air pressure builds up, and finally the "burst" in which the lips are opened and the sudden release of pressure makes a sound. For a singer, the process described above is literally the technique used to sing (or articulate) a "P." Wind players apply some of the same techniques used in speaking, although they mostly use the tongue, not the lips, for articulation (in speech, the tongue is used to pronounce "T" or "D," gentler articulations than "P"). String players use their bow to stop and start the vibration of the strings; their right hand creates motions that correspond to the action of the tongue or lips in speaking. And on the piano we use the hammers and the dampers to start and stop our notes. But we have nothing analogous to the buildup of pressure that produces the "P" sound. When singing or speaking, we can make the "P" itself strong or gentle at any volume level, from a whisper to a shout. So can the wind player, or the string player, but not the pianist. At any piano, we can only increase the force of that initial impact by making the hammer go faster, and that makes the entire note louder.

The Two-Note Slur

Two-note slurs are ubiquitous in the classical style. Example 3.10 has one in every measure (except m. 3, which has two):

Example 3.10. Haydn, Sonata in F major, Hob. XVI:23, mvt. 3, mm. 1–8.

Consider the slur between f¹ and e¹ in measure 2. As discussed in Chapter 2, slurs require three things from the performer:

1. connection (legato or over-legato) between the notes;
2. stress on the first note;
3. release on the last note (i.e., shortening and lightening).

This is a very easy gesture to sing, with a strongly stressed first note and a very gentle, short second note. I use the syllables "tee–ya": "t" makes a strong attack on the first note, and "y" produces the smooth transition between the two vowels (whose counterparts are the two notes in the music). It's also a very straightforward figure to play on the fortepiano, because the first note's quick diminuendo naturally prepares a softer second note, which is then gently stopped by the damper. The effect is that of a single sound with a pitch change, just like the vowel change on either side of the "y." On the modern piano, however, the second note has to be just right: too soft, and it gets lost; too loud, and the release sounds clipped. The slurs in the odd-numbered bars don't present this problem, since clipping the second note suits the lively, jumpy theme. But in the even-numbered bars, a bit of extra time (unnecessary at the fortepiano) may help convey the gentle release at the end of each gesture. With clear articulation in measures 2, 4, and 6 we hear four self-contained two-measure units; without them, the music continues straight through without breathing for eight bars. And although those eight bars do constitute a single phrase, it's the short breaths—panting, almost—that convey the theme's character.

Sometimes, composers used specific notational devices to suggest different ways of releasing two-note gestures. In Example 3.11, Mozart notates the same motive in two ways:

Example 3.11. Mozart, Sonata in C major, K. 309, mvt. 1, mm. 35–42.

It's possible that no difference was intended, and that Mozart only omitted the rests in measures 41–42 out of laziness or carelessness. Or perhaps they were redundant to begin with, since the sources tell us that the last note under a slur was always shortened. In that case, Mozart may have written the rests just to make sure we separate the figures, then expected us to remember to do the same thing four bars later. But if so, why does he make the same distinction again at the recapitulation (mm. 129–36)?

I'd rather draw the opposite conclusion: Mozart wants to make sure that we play the second four bars differently, and he shows us how to do it. The motive is lighter the first time (because of the rests) and heavier the second time, creating a link to the next, stronger phrase (mm. 43ff.). The strokes for the left hand in measure 42 are also part of this plan, as are the new pitches: e^2–d^2 instead of b^1–a^1 in the melody. Following Mozart's hints I play measures 35–38 gently and playfully, and measures 39–42 with determination and a crescendo.

The Multiple-Note Slur

According to Leopold Mozart, every slur, no matter how many notes it covers, should be played diminuendo, with an emphasis on the first note.[18] This rule is very broad, and as with any broad statement, there are bound to be exceptions. C. P. E. Bach's discussion of slurs points out the interaction of this rule with the demands of metrical accentuation: "patterns of two and four slurred notes are played with a slight, scarcely noticeable increase of pressure on the first and third tones."[19] Melodic contour and rhythmic factors also influence the dynamic shape, as in Example 3.12. Here I follow Leopold Mozart's prescription for the three-note slurs in measures 5 and 7,

Example 3.12. Mozart, Sonata in F major, K. 332, mvt. 1, mm. 5–8.

but in measures 6 and 8 the second-beat C gets more stress because of its pitch and its length.

Successive Slurs

Much anxiety has been caused by the short slurs at the beginning of K. 332 and similar passages. As we saw in Chapter 1, some nineteenth-century editors eliminated them, replacing them with a single long slur to indicate phrasing. The eighteenth century's taste for articulated performance was simply erased; a thoughtful player working from the Schirmer edition (Example 1.1, p. 4) would never know that such a style even existed.

In their definitive book on Mozart performance, Paul and Eva Badura-Skoda decry this practice.[20] They say, "Mozart never used slurs in his music as phrasing marks," yet they are unwilling to accept the implication that the slurs must, therefore, indicate articulation. They divide Mozart's slurs into two types: "articulating slurs" (these are the usual slurs) and "legato slurs," which they claim were used "[to] indicate legato over a fairly long section, which, however, Mozart usually wrote with slurs lasting only one measure each *in accordance with established practice*" (emphasis mine). And yet they quote this very example, in which the left hand's two-measure slur (mm. 1–2) in Mozart's autograph (Example 1.2, p. 4) provides a counterexample to "established practice."[21]

Like many musicians, the Badura-Skodas sense that the notation is significant, but are unconvinced by the musical result of carrying it out. Their ambivalence can be seen in their advice for performing this passage from the original 1957 edition of their book: "In passages such as these, one should try to lift the hand from the keys a little at the end of the slur, while maintaining a legato with the pedal."[22]

For the revised version of the book, published in 2008 (more than fifty years later!), they take quite a different approach. This time they propose singing the passage to an invented text whose words can serve as a guide or inspiration when playing at the keyboard. These bars are given two texts, one in Italian and one in English, which—at least when I sing them—produce quite different results. The English words are "Come and play and sing with pleasure!," and the Badura-Skodas' commentary appears rather to relate to the Italian words: *Canta, canta, con passione!*[23] As the authors wrote, "The comma after the first and second measures comes quite naturally. It leads to an ever so slight interruption of the air flow, yet no new breath is taken until the end of this melody."[24]

I agree with this interpretation completely, and it is not difficult to produce the analog of *Canta, Canta* on the fortepiano, where a subtle gap between the slurs is clearly discernible, eloquent and expressive. I do it without pedal, but use finger-pedal in the left hand to enrich the harmony while preserving the articulation in the right hand. Creating the same effect on the modern piano is more challenging. Simply lifting the finger as I do on the fortepiano creates a release that is far too abrupt for this passage. But using the pedal to maintain the legato, as the Badura-Skodas suggested in their original publication, obscures the delicate expression. With the fortepiano's version firmly in mind, I find that a slow release of the second note, together with (if it sounds too dry) a brief, very shallow pedal, produces an effect that is very similar: the elusive, "ever so slight interruption of the air flow." As in the repeated notes of Example 3.9, what's required, and too rarely cultivated by pianists, is a virtuoso command of the dampers equal to that of the hammers.

Some players—taking advantage of the modern piano's capability for continuous, sustained lines—may even use the pedal to connect the short slurs in measures 105 and 107 of Example 3.13, despite the dramatic contrasts of register and dynamic. Surely the gaps are the essence of this passage!

Slur+1

Classical composers frequently end a slur just before the final note of a motive or phrase. This situation is not very different from the previous examples, only with a single note in place of another slur. Again, a gentle release at the end of the slur, meticulous control of dynamics, and a judicious, subtle articulation will generally produce a very satisfying effect, even on the modern piano. Nevertheless, nineteenth-century editors often "corrected" the text by extending the slur to include the final note, as in the Schirmer edition of K. 283 (compare Example 3.14 with Mozart's notation in Example 3.3).

Mozart's intentions seem clear. The piece begins with two contrasting figures: the first (d^2–b^1– d^2) is a "normal" one with an articulated downbeat; the second (g^1–$f\sharp^1$) features an unusual slur over the barline that displaces

Example 3.13. Mozart, Sonata in C major, K. 309, mvt. 1, mm. 103–8.

Example 3.14. Mozart, Sonata in G major, K.283, mvt. 1, mm. 1–7 (Schirmer edition).

the accent, giving the figure a sly or insinuating character. The editor assumes that the pianist is incapable of performing the subtle articulation at the beginning (admittedly easier to do on the fortepiano than on the modern piano), and instead slurs the three notes together and adds an accent (>) sign on the last note—a combination unknown in Mozart's notation. Having created this un-Mozartean gesture of an end-accented slur, he then feels obliged to add a dot to the end of the next slur, in order to remind us of how a "real" slur works.

In the opening of Mozart's sonata K. 533 (Example 3.15), slur+1 plays a particularly subtle role:

The first phrase is composed of a two-measure idea and its nearly identical repetition. While the second half of the phrase presents a textbook example of slur+1, the relationship between the first two measures is more complicated. In both cases, the eight-note slurred figure is certainly incomplete without the following f¹. But, if the first slur were extended to include the first note of the following measure, the next idea would appear to begin with

Example 3.15. Mozart, Sonata in F major, K. 533, mvt. 1, mm. 1–4.

Example 3.16. Mozart, Sonata in F major, K. 533, mvt. 1, mm. 49–51.

the octave leap c^1–c^2. This would be consistent with the new continuation that appears at measures 49–50, shown in Example 3.16.

Measure 2 can also be read differently. Divide it down the middle, so that the first gesture includes both f^1 and c^1. Now the c^2 introduces a repeat of the opening figure (with the first note elongated), and the opening gesture matches the form Mozart gives it at the beginning of the development section (Example 3.17):

Example 3.17. Mozart, Sonata in F major, K. 533, mvt. 1, mm. 103–5.

Seen this way, the tiny articulation at the barline between measures 1 and 2 is critical, permitting the first note of measure 2 to serve both as the resolution of e^1, and the beginning of a new two-note figure (which Mozart will transform in mm. 105ff.).

In a dense, provocative essay entitled "Phrasing in Contention," the clarinetist Anthony Pay argues that classical-style slurs represent the

Example 3.18. Mozart, Sonata in B-flat major, K. 333, mvt. 1, mm. 111–12.

ornamentation of a single pitch, and—if performed correctly—the listener should be able to perceive them that way. I find it helpful, when practicing, to actually replace the slurred groups with single notes. Try it with Example 3.18, replacing c^2–a^1 in measures 111 and 112 with a longer c^2. (In a clever touch, Pay considers the stroke a "one-note slur," which gives the "+1" notes the same weight as a slurred group.)

But why so much fuss? Why not simply treat the longer shapes as a continuous line? I consider Mozart's technique of constructing phrases from delicately balanced smaller units the hallmark of his style. The projection of those units and the exquisite relationships among them constitutes—for me—the principal challenge of playing his music. Everyone's taste is different: what sounds eloquent to me may sound contrived and fussy to you. Taste in declamation also changes over time, as one can easily see by watching old movies, political speeches, or comedy routines. The concern for continuity, and the potential for disturbing it by over-articulating, is not new: Beethoven reportedly found Mozart's style choppy,[25] and Türk warned his readers not to interrupt a musical idea by taking the hands off the keys before reaching the end of a thought.[26] But today's players generally emphasize the bigger picture; I'm interested in the details that are often overlooked.

Ordinary Touch

Here is a concise description by Marpurg: "Normal onward movement is the opposite of both slurring and detaching: it consists of lifting the finger nimbly from the preceding key just before one touches the next one. This normal onward movement was always taken for granted, was never indicated."[27] C. P. E. Bach seems to be recommending the same thing with his critical, condescending prose:

> Some persons play too stickily, as if they had glue between their fingers; their touch is too long, because they keep the keys down beyond the time. Others

have attempted to avoid this defect and play too short, as if the keys were burning hot. This is also a fault. The middle path is the best.[28]

On the fortepiano it's easy to differentiate among legato, staccato, and "ordinary touch." Mozart sometimes highlights the contrast between touches, as in Example 3.19 (note both the thirty-second notes and the triplets):

Example 3.19. Mozart, Adagio in B minor, K. 540, mm. 46–49.

One of my students declared that this was *the* defining quality of the fortepiano. He wrote: "the ordinary touch, this non-legato sonority, is what characterizes the fortepiano and makes it totally different from the modern piano." On the fortepiano, with its extremely shallow key dip, the non-legato touch emerges with ease simply by aiming for the surface of the keys, just grazing them (in contrast to legato, where I focus on the bottom of the stroke). At the modern piano it's harder to project non-legato without calling undue attention to the effort of separating the notes. It's a subtle effect, easy to overdo. As a technical aid, I try to picture two adjacent keys as one is falling and one is rising: if they pass each other near the bottom of the stroke the sounds will be connected; if higher up, we will hear non-legato.

Playing Music Not Written Specifically for the Piano

Harpsichord music normally has no dynamic indications,[29] but, as pianos became more common, composers began to add dynamics to make their music seem up-to-date and, perhaps, more attractive to owners of the trendy new instrument. At least one composer made this explicit. The Paris-based

Johann Gottlieb Eckard included this explanation in the preface to his sonatas, published as Opus 1 in 1763: "I set out to make this work equally useful
at the harpsichord, clavichord, and fortepiano. This is why I felt obliged to
indicate the softs and louds so frequently, which would have been pointless
had I been concerned only with the harpsichord."[30]

For composers concerned primarily with the harpsichord (including
Haydn into his maturity) the principal strategies for varying the intensity
were *texture, ornamentation, register*, and *articulation*.

Texture and dynamics are independent features of the musical fabric, but
they are closely related: more notes = more sound. This is true in the vertical
dimension (a chord makes more sound than a single note) and in the horizontal dimension (more notes per unit of time = more sound). Ornaments
such as trills, mordents, and *acciaccature*, by their addition of extra notes,
emphasize selected pitches even on an instrument where they cannot be
played louder. Register can be a stand-in for dynamics: the lower registers
are louder because there is more energy in the longer, heavier strings and the
sound is richer in overtones, while the upper registers seem less substantial,
thinner. Articulation, too, has a dynamic component. The beginning of a
slur is heard clearly and sounds louder; subsequent attacks are covered by the
still-sounding previous note.

Of course, a pianist can choose to play chords or trills quietly and single
notes loudly, or play a slur crescendo instead of diminuendo, just as composers, writing for the piano, could ask for these effects explicitly. But in repertoire composed for a "generic" keyboard, the musical language is subject to
the instruments' inherent characteristics. Even on a clavichord, where the
player controls the level of individual notes, texture still plays a major role in
determining the loudness of a passage. The same is still true, to some extent,
on the early piano. We can see how it works in a sonata by Haydn from 1780
(Example 3.20).

The chords in the left hand produce accents on the downbeats: a stronger
one with the four-note chord in the lower register in the first bar, then a
weaker one with the three-note chord in a softer register in the second bar.
The ornaments in the right hand also stress the first, third, and fourth beats.
In the third measure, the slurs in the outer voices reinforce the syncopation
in the alto voice to create lively, off-beat accents. Changing the accompaniment also provides dynamic variety. The Alberti bass beginning at measure 5
softens the downbeat accents at the beginning of the phrase, while the added
sixths in the right hand at measure 8 together with the left hand's descent
into the lower register add weight to the cadence. Register contrast can create

Example 3.20. Haydn, Sonata in D major, Hob. XVI:37, mvt. 1, mm. 1–16.

an echo effect, as in measures 9–12; the upper octave sounds softer. And playing octaves in the two hands suggests the full sound of an orchestral *tutti*, as Haydn does at the cadence (mm. 14–16).

A keyboard player brought up according to Bach's prescription—playing pieces like this one interchangeably on the harpsichord and clavichord—would have had no trouble making sense of the music on either instrument. Haydn's design creates dynamic contrasts at the harpsichord automatically; at the clavichord these could be reinforced by the player's touch.

At the piano the lack of dynamic instructions appears to give the player *carte blanche*: one could, for example, begin measure 9 *pianissimo* and crescendo through the entire passage. But, treating Haydn's choices of texture and register as indicative of his wishes, the downbeat of measure 9 with its octave in the bass should be strongly accented, the repeat in the upper register similar but somewhat weaker, and a crescendo could begin with the octave doubling at measure 15.

In addition to these hints from the texture, an eighteenth-century musician would have taken into account two other factors influencing dynamics: meter and harmony. Meter is a pervasive factor, affecting not only the strong beats of the measure but also the smaller subdivisions. Obviously, we cannot be expected to accent the first and third note of every group of four sixteenth notes, but a clear projection of the meter is essential. Similarly, harmony makes its own claims. Dissonances should be louder than their resolutions; dominant harmony is normally stronger than tonic. And although the melodic principle—more intensity when the notes rise and less when they fall—certainly operates across a broad range of styles, in pre-Romantic repertoire it is often subservient to the demands of meter and harmony.

These factors also operate in later pieces like Mozart's sonata K. 570 (clearly written for the piano, but with few dynamic indications) where we can still infer the composer's intentions from his handling of texture and register. In Example 3.21, the texture initially supports the meter: the chord in measure 21 guarantees that the first beat will sound heavier than the second. Subsequently, Mozart changes the placement of the chord, creating the opposite effect. While it is possible to fight the texture and register by stressing the first beat and lightening the second beat here as well, the result is very unnatural, and almost certainly the opposite of what Mozart expected.

Early Dynamic Markings

As noted earlier, the sonatas in Mozart's first collection, K. 279–284 (ca. 1775), contain many dynamic indications, unlike Haydn's works from the same period. Perhaps Mozart wanted to urge players to take advantage of the dynamic resources of the new and unfamiliar fortepiano, since his later

Example 3.21. Mozart, Sonata in B-flat major, K. 570, mvt. 1, mm. 21–22, 39–40.

works rarely contain so many markings so close together. Some of the early instructions can be vexing, especially at a modern piano. Several points to bear in mind:

Example 3.22. Mozart, Sonata in F major, K. 280, mvt. 1, mm. 27–31.

Firstly, some markings simply confirm features in the texture that already create dynamic contrast; the player needn't belabor the obvious. The octaves in measures 27 and 31 of Example 3.22 are intrinsically *forte*; played too loudly they can easily become caricature, especially on a modern piano.

Likewise the effect of the *f* chords and the *p* thirds at measure 75 (Example 3.23) will be largely accomplished by the contrast in register and texture.

Example 3.23. Mozart, Sonata in F major, K. 280, mvt. 1, mm. 75–78.

In Example 3.24, contrasting articulations, rather than textures, are associated with different dynamic levels (staccato with *f*, slurs with *p*).

Example 3.24. Mozart, Sonata in F major, K. 280, mvt. 1, mm. 122–26.

It's as though the two kinds of instructions are aimed at two sets of per-formers: pianists may convey the sense of the passage primarily through the dynamics, while harpsichordists depend more on the contrasting articula-tions. (At a two-manual harpsichord the contrast could also be heightened with a change of keyboard.) Mozart uses the same technique elsewhere in the movement. When the material from measures 27–28 (Example 3.22) reappears in the development section, the sixteenth notes are no longer *p* and slurred but *f* and separate. The change in articulation is easy to overlook (some might think it simply an oversight), but the combination of both ele-ments is highly effective at the fortepiano, and worth cultivating at the mod-ern piano as well.

Even when making a purely dynamic effect, players would probably still have used other techniques to reinforce the contrast. In measures 63–66 of Example 3.25, the left hand's quarter notes could be made longer in measure 63, and shorter in measure 65 (but definitely not legato in either spot).

Example 3.25. Mozart, Sonata in F major, K. 280, mvt. 1, mm. 61–66.

Secondly, since Mozart rarely indicated crescendo and diminuendo in these works, the transition between dynamic levels could be gradual rather than sudden. Thus in a passage like Example 3.26, the *f* bars could be played diminuendo, with a natural decay beginning during the trill.

Example 3.26. Mozart, Sonata in B-flat major, K. 281, mvt. 3, mm. 18–21.

Finally, there is ample reason to suspect that, in this music, *f* is not *so* loud, and *p* is not *so* soft. These pieces predate Mozart's October 1777 favorable encounter with Stein's pianos in Augsburg; before that, as he wrote to his father, Späth had been his favorite. All the surviving instruments by Späth are *Tangentenflügel*, on which it is difficult to play soft (because of the hard surface of the jack) and dangerous to play too loud (because it's easy to cause the jack to rebound and hit the string twice, causing an unpleasant "chattering" sound). Typical square pianos of the period have similar limitations. Consequently, the contrast between *f* and *p* could be relatively subtle—as suggested by Leopold Mozart's use of the terms "light and shade" in his violin treatise.

Damper "Pedal"

Of the "many kinds of keyboard instruments" used in the eighteenth century, only pianos had a mechanism for raising all of the dampers together. Early square pianos (and some grands as well[31]) offered a hand stop for this purpose; most Viennese grand pianos from this period use a knee lever. For most pianists, pedaling with the thigh (the "knee lever" is actually located under the keyboard) is initially shocking, but easy to get used to. Nevertheless, it remains clumsier to use than an actual pedal, and I am convinced that the constant pedaling we take for granted today was not practiced with this type of mechanism. Once players began to use the damper lifter as a regular part of playing technique, builders accommodated them by adopting a foot-operated mechanism. This happened after 1805 in Vienna, earlier in London.

With a generous use of overholding or "finger-pedal"— sometimes called "prolonged touch" or *legatissimo* in the sources—most eighteenth-century piano music can be played without pedal, at least on the fortepiano.[32] When, then, did Mozart use the pedal? He certainly was aware of it, as we see from this letter to his father praising Stein's pianos, in 1777: "The thing that you press with your knee is also better made by him than by others. I barely move it, and it works; and as soon as you take the knee away, even a little bit, you don't hear the slightest reverberation."[33] Unfortunately, this is the only direct evidence that we have about Mozart's use of the pedal. Maybe C. P. E. Bach provides a clue in this passage from the chapter of the *Versuch* that deals with improvisation: "The best instruments for our purpose are the clavichord and pianoforte. Both can and must be well tuned. The undamped register of the pianoforte is the most pleasing and, once the performer learns to observe the necessary precautions in the face of its reverberations, the most delightful for improvisation."[34]

It's easy to imagine that Mozart also found improvising with the "undamped register" delightful. I've chosen excerpts from the fantasies in D minor and C minor (Examples 3.27 and 3.28) that suggest written-out improvisations. The proposed pedaling underlines the harmonic progressions on which they are based (this is the "rhythmic pedal" described in Chapter 2).

Other "Pedals"

Although five-octave Viennese pianos did not have a shift (*una corda*) mechanism, some had another kind of "soft pedal," the *moderator*. It works by

Example 3.27. Mozart, Fantasy in D minor, K. 397, mm. 1–11 (pedaling added).

Example 3.28. Mozart, Fantasy in C minor, K. 475, mm. 6–12 (pedaling added).

sliding a strip of cloth between the hammers and the strings, producing a dark, veiled sonority that contrasts strongly with the relatively bright sound of the fortepiano. This makes it a powerful resource but also limits its use, since it is virtually impossible to make a smooth transition in or out of its special sound. In this respect it is much more like a string player's mute than like the *una corda* of the modern piano. (On some pianos the moderator is controlled by a hand stop instead of a knee lever. This makes it even more like a mute, because a free hand is needed to operate it.) Although no major eighteenth-century composer called for it explicitly, it can create an atmosphere of profound melancholy for pieces like the slow movement of Haydn's Hob. XVI:23, or make a dramatic echo effect for short repeated sections, or give the impression of music vanishing into the distance, as at the end of Mozart's K. 330 or Haydn's F minor variations.

Putting It All Together: A Case Study

To see how these ideas work in practice, here is a comprehensive look at the first movement of Mozart's Sonata in E-flat, K. 282 (Example 3.29).

Example 3.29. Mozart, Sonata in E-flat major, K. 282, mvt. 1, mm. 1–9.

Tempo and Rhythm

Tempo choice is pivotal, affecting virtually every other aspect of performance. The long tones of the modern piano make it possible to play slow pieces at speeds that would have been unimaginable to their composers; the quick decay of the fortepiano's tones limits how slowly one can play a movement like this one convincingly. On my Walter copy, for my ears, that limit is ♩ = M.M. 40, although I find 42–44 more comfortable. Many recorded performances on the modern piano fall within that range. However, I found a few strikingly slower versions:[35] beautiful in their way, but inconceivable on any piano Mozart would have known.

With the somewhat quicker, more flexible tempo inspired by the fortepiano, I like to follow Leopold Mozart's advice for the opening figure, overdotting slightly to keep the rhythm from sounding sluggish (see p. 15). This also makes the relationship with measure 16—technically a strict diminution of the original—clearer to the listener, by giving the short c^2s a more similar duration (compare Examples 3.29 and 3.35).

Texture and Polyphony

The sheer beauty of the melody at the modern piano might lead us to overlook the polyphonic qualities of this movement, starting with the bass line that descends stepwise through an entire octave in the first four bars. Don't miss it! And bringing out all the parts in measure 8 enhances the seriousness of the "learned style" (an allusion to old-fashioned counterpoint that Schumann and Brahms use for the same purpose) before the light-hearted, *galant* style enters in measure 9.

Dynamic Indications

This movement begins without any dynamic indication. Some editors add *f*, either on the basis of the subsequent *p*, or because various treatises recommend *f* as the "default" dynamic for the beginning of a piece.[36] Other editors, like Lebert, supply *p*, which is harder to justify. I think Mozart trusts us to do something reasonable here—neither too loud nor too soft—while the *p* at measure 4 is essential, because the natural response to the increased activity in the left hand would be to get louder.

Between measures 4 and 9 we find the profusion of markings alluded to on pp. 25 and 47. In the autograph they make an even more striking impression, because Mozart uses the longer forms *"pia:"* and *"for:"* and writes them independently in each hand, for a total of nineteen directions in six measures! Leopold Mozart's description of dynamics as "light and shade" makes the alternation of *p* and *f* in these measures more understandable, since light and shade suggest a range: they can be very sharply contrasted, as in bright sunlight, or relatively subtle. Later composers show these gradations with the range of symbols *ppp–pp–p–mp–mf–f–ff–fff*; Mozart leaves the "dosage" up to us.

Besides the degree of contrast, one must also decide on the nature of the transitions. Recall that Leopold Mozart also wrote, "one must know *how* [emphasis mine] to change from *piano* to *forte* without directions and of one's own accord." Although Mozart occasionally writes *crescendo* (mm. 17 and 19 of this very movement), we shouldn't assume that a *subito* effect is expected in all other cases. In this respect, too, later composers (especially Beethoven) are more explicit, but for Haydn, Mozart, or C. P. E. Bach it is important to consider each passage individually. For example, I favor a diminuendo in the second half of measures 4 and 5, a shape that is also supported by the slurs.

The *f–p* markings for the left hand at measure 9 and the corresponding spot in measure 27 are a special case, and to understand them requires an investigation into Mozart's accompaniment patterns. In Mozart's early sonatas and concertos the accompaniments are generally patterns of single notes (including the Alberti type) or repeated chords; Example 3.30 neatly displays all of these styles.

Example 3.30. Mozart, Sonata in F major, K. 280, mvt. 1, mm. 1–9.

In the measure under consideration the texture works against the meter. On each beat a bass note is played alone but on the off-beats two notes are sounded together—the only instance of this pattern in Mozart's piano sonatas. When he does something similar in later pieces, he gives the bass note a longer value, as in Example 3.31:

Example 3.31. Mozart, Trio in E-flat major, K. 498, mvt. 3, mm. 49–51 (other parts are silent).

Or, as in this well-known case ("Rondo alla turca," Example 3.32), the bass note is lengthened and stressed because of the slur.

Example 3.32. Mozart, Sonata in A major, K. 331, mvt. 3, mm. 1–2.

Mozart's accompaniments show great imagination and variety. If at this time he was experimenting with the new possibilities offered by the piano ("he plays differently from how he did in Salzburg"), we should expect new kinds of accompanimental figures too. The compound accompaniment we find at measure 9 of K. 282, in which the left hand plays both a distinct bass and a middle voice or voices, is made possible by the piano's ability to bring out the bass notes and put the middle voice into the background, a resource that is unavailable at the harpsichord.[37] The dynamic indications may simply indicate how to handle this novel, specifically pianistic texture. The *fortes* could be calibrated in accordance with the meter: strongest on the first beat, least on beats two and four, a gentle emphasis on three. The bass notes could also be lengthened somewhat—but not slurred into the following notes, which would transform this unusual accompaniment into one of the patterns cited above.

Articulation

At the modern piano the opening of this piece is usually played with continuous legato, aided by a generous use of the pedal. This enhances the beauty of the melody, and gives the opening a serene character that is much more difficult to achieve on the fortepiano. But judging by his directions, Mozart may not have had this sort of performance in mind: the first three bars alone contain six distinct two-note slurs (seven if you count the one implied by the appoggiatura at the beginning of m. 2), and the next four bars have six breaks in the sound indicated by rests. At the fortepiano, these articulations can be performed comfortably, adding interest and life to the music. At the modern piano it's challenging to do so without sounding too choppy: to justify the struggle, we need to understand the role of these details in Mozart's design:

1. The most important break is in the middle of measure 2; I've indicated this with a comma (see Example. 3.29). A clear articulation between the d^2 and the preceding bb^1 clarifies the phrasing, and also emphasizes the poignant dissonance between d^2 in the right hand and e^1 in the left.

2. The c^2–bb^1 slur at the beginning of measure 3 is a sequential repetition of the d^2–c^2 in the previous bar; separating the two slurs f^2–d^2 and c^2–bb^1 reveals this sequence and heightens the expressive value of the dissonant c^2. With the space before f^2–d^2 I try to show how the three-note motive d^2–c^2–c^2 has been expanded into a five-note figure with the addition of the upbeats. Similarly, a space before eb^2 in the middle of measure 3 sets off the third step in the downward progression. That adds up to a lot of spaces, but if we are willing to give up a seamless surface, each of them contributes to the complexity and expressivity of the music.

3. The same applies to the rests in measures 4–7. Many pianists cover these with the pedal (perhaps without realizing it) which certainly makes for a smoother line. But observing the rests underscores the halting nature of this phrase, first rising hopefully (g^2 and ab^2 are the highest pitches so far, emphasized by the slides and the *fs*) then falling back, defeatedly, in the minor mode. And don't overlook the articulation of the final dissonant cry—eb^2 against $e\natural$ in measure 7; the stroke on the preceding c^2 suggests that even the usual amount of articulation is not enough!

4. The opening gesture, a slur+1, is difficult to play naturally, even on the fortepiano. Why not continue the slur to the third note, as recommended by Sigmund Lebert in his edition (Example 3.33)?

Example 3.33 Mozart, Sonata in E-flat major, K. 282, mvt. 1, mm. 1–3 (Carl Fischer edition).

Taking a cue from Anthony Pay's theory that a slurred group represents the ornamentation of a single pitch (discussed on pp. 42–43), we could reduce the opening bars to the version shown in Example 3.34.

Example 3.34. Mozart, Sonata in E-flat major, K. 282, mvt. 1, mm. 1–2, reduction.

In this reduction we are obliged to articulate the second bb^1, since the key must be released before it can be repeated, and that articulation makes the syncopation clear. When performing the music as written, a well-defined performance of the slur+1 preserves that structure. The first three notes certainly form one gesture, but they don't have to be played legato. If all three are slurred, the underlying structure is reduced to a single long note, and the syncopation disappears.

Try this exercise: First, become comfortable with the "simplified" version and the articulation that it produces (as long as you aren't pedaling through the repeated notes). Then try adding the c^2 (softly) while overholding the bb^1, and releasing both simultaneously before the second beat. I would perform the figure just like that, but you may prefer to remove some or all of the overlap.

Treating the first gesture as a syncopation not only makes the opening more interesting, it also prepares the listener for the syncopations in measure 3 (these are at the next level down metrically: ♪–♩, instead of ♩–♩). This analysis might seem overly subtle, but look at measures 16–17 (Example 3.35):

Example 3.35. Mozart, Sonata in E-flat major, K. 282, mvt. 1, mm. 16–18.

Here the opening motive has been transformed rhythmically so that the syncopation is at the eighth-note level, as in measure 3. The quicker note values allow Mozart to syncopate two beats in succession, with the octave leap making the second one especially prominent. He goes one step further in measure 17 with four syncopated beats in succession, reinforced by a crescendo and added appoggiaturas. In the coda (Example 3.36), all of these strands come together: The original rhythm returns, but the rearticulation of the bb^1 makes this syncopation even more prominent.

Example 3.36. Mozart, Sonata in E-flat major, K. 282, mvt. 1, mm. 34–36.

Ordinary Touch

Consider the notation of the pairs of sixteenth notes in measure 2 (refer to Example 3.29). First comes the "small-note" notation of the appoggiatura $eb^2–d^2$, then two unmarked notes, $c^2–bb^1$, then the two slurred pairs $d^2–c^2$ and $f^2–d^2$, followed by two more pairs in the next measure. I carefully articulate the two-note slurs, but use "ordinary touch" (i.e., non-legato) for the unmarked notes, in order to highlight the difference between the two otherwise identical figures circled in Example 3.29. Although this sounds (and feels) perfectly natural on the fortepiano, it can easily be overdone at the modern piano. But these subtle distinctions make the difference between "speaking" and "singing" the opening bars.

Prolonged Touch ("Finger-Pedal")

The left-hand part in measures 4–7 presents the "curved line over harmonies which are to be slowly arpeggiated," as described by Türk. Without pedal the accompaniment sounds thin and unconvincing, but adding it masks the rests in the right-hand part. Türk tells us that in such cases "it is customary, … to let the fingers remain on the keys until the appearance of the next harmony." Make sure that the first note of each slur is also gently stressed, bringing out the bass line. Using finger-pedal in this passage also maximizes the contrast between the hands: the left hand as "gluey" and continuous as possible; the right hand tentative, interrupted by rests.

Slurs and Dynamic Shapes

The right hand's motive in measure 9 (see Example 3.29) consists of seven notes: a rising three-note slur, followed by four descending notes. The usual "modern" way of expressing the first slur is to make the three notes lead to the middle of the bar (i.e., crescendo). According to Leopold Mozart's rule we should do the opposite and play these three notes diminuendo. Each approach has disadvantages: the crescendo detracts from the stress I want to give the appoggiatura, and the diminuendo undermines the close connection among the seven notes of the figure. Gently underplaying the first f^2 gives me the best of both worlds. Care is required to avoid making the space between the two f^2s too large, but I prefer a somewhat fussily articulated version to a heaving, accordion-like swell.

The longer the slur, the more likely it is that Leopold Mozart's "rule of diminuendo" may come into conflict with other principles, but those in Example 3.37—especially those marked f—respond well to this shape.

Example 3.37. Mozart, Sonata in E-flat major, K. 282, mvt. 1, mm. 15, 20.

We end our examination of this movement with measure 8, the most complicated spot in the piece. The left hand has "normal" slurs, reinforcing the meter, while the right hand's unusual articulation weakens the c^2 ("rule of diminuendo") and accentuates the $e\natural^2$ (first note of a slur). The complexity of these details and the density of the harmonic motion make *rubato* and *ritardando* virtually inevitable, giving this measure the heightened expression that is its due.

English Pianos and Haydn's Last Sonatas

We turn now to some exceptional pieces—the sonatas Haydn composed during his visits to London. The pianos he encountered there were quite different from the ones at home: those by English builders such as Broadwood had a less sensitive, heavier action, and a longer-lasting, mellower tone than contemporary Viennese instruments. They also had relatively light, inefficient dampers, which surrounded the sound with a halo of "after-ring." English pianos were already equipped with actual pedals operated by the feet, while the Viennese still used knee levers. Overall, English pianos had a thicker, more resonant sound than the Viennese, while individual tones were less detailed and articulated. Correspondingly, English piano music was characterized by more symphonic textures, greater use of the pedal, and a preference for legato.

Music by eighteenth-century English composers isn't played very much,[38] but most pianists know at least one of the sonatas Haydn composed in England. Haydn had made a point of telling Johann Peter Salomon, the impresario who invited him, that he would not compose the requested new symphonies until after he arrived in London and could understand the English taste.[39] So it's reasonable to imagine that the keyboard pieces he wrote in England for English patrons (three sonatas, and perhaps as many as seven of the piano trios) were similarly tailored to the pianos he found there. The C major sonata has two such attributes: it calls for notes above the range of the standard Viennese piano (g^3 and a^3), and it includes two spots with explicit pedaling directions (the only pedal indications in all of Haydn's works, shown in Example 3.38), using the then common English term "*open pedal*" for the damper pedal.

Similar passages in works by Clementi, Dussek, and others suggest that this kind of "messy" blurring of harmonies was popular, and it produces an attractive sound on most early pianos. Recreating this effect on a modern piano requires subtle partial changes of the pedal—but not to the point of

Example 3.38. Haydn, Sonata in C major, Hob. XVI:50, mvt. 1, mm. 73–74.

cleaning it up entirely! Beethoven was also influenced by English pianos and pianists; his "messy pedaling" will be examined in the next chapter.

Rapid parallel thirds are common in Clementi's sonatas, and we can find them in each of Haydn's London sonatas.[40] They are very idiomatic on English pianos, because the "halo" created by the light damping makes them relatively smooth even when played non-legato. In measures 3–5 of the E-flat sonata (Example 3.39) we find thirds both soft and loud, slurred and unslurred.[41]

The first group of four are *piano,* and slurred. The longer series (upbeat to m. 5) begins with these same four notes, still slurred but now *forte,* then continues unslurred. I make the variety of articulation a primary property of the passage, playing the slurred notes as smoothly as possible with a true legato fingering in the top voice, and using a rattling, brilliant non-legato for the rest. It sounds terrific on an English piano, but the Viennese piano does it well, too. Some fancy pedaling—very shallow with fairly quick changes—may be necessary on a modern piano to compensate for the dryness, but the distinction between legato and non-legato is worth the effort. (Warning: some older editions put a long slur over all of m. 5!)

Our modern pianos have inherited many characteristics from the English instruments of that time, so it isn't really surprising that Haydn's English

Example 3.39. Haydn, Sonata in E-flat major, Hob. XVI:52, mvt. 1, mm. 3–5.

sonatas are the most frequently played today.[42] Their thicker textures, designed expressly for the pianos he found in London, are also well suited to our modern ones. But this is no reason to ignore the others! Haydn certainly considered all of his keyboard music suitable for both English and Viennese pianos. The sonatas he composed in London were also published in Vienna,[43] and the earlier, "non-English" pieces were obviously played in England, on English pianos: it's because Haydn was already famous in England that he was invited to travel there in the first place.

Ensemble Music

The use of period pianos in chamber music has an additional impact because the balance between instruments has changed dramatically: the piano has transformed enormously over the past two centuries compared to the changes made to other instruments. Classical composers could regard the fortepianist's hands as two ensemble members, the equivalent of a violin or flute and a cello; C. P. E. Bach actually called his sonatas for keyboard plus one instrument "Trios." The timbres are similar enough that the instruments can comfortably exchange parts, or play in parallel thirds or sixths. Mozart, in his violin sonatas, usually treats the piano's right hand as just another violin; each takes turns playing the role of "first" or "second." It's no wonder that, in the eighteenth century, these pieces were called *Accompanied Keyboard Sonatas*. The piano was not doing the accompanying; it was being accompanied—expanded and extended—*by* the other instruments.

The modern piano, on the other hand, is more like an entire orchestra. It can accompany another instrument, or complement it in any number of ways, but the listener will never be in doubt as to who is playing what. Paradoxically, modern pianists playing a violin or cello sonata sound more like accompanists than their counterparts at the quieter fortepiano, because they create a more unified, homogeneous texture against which the other instrument sounds like a soloist. Also, it is hard to disguise the fact that the modern pianist cannot use the full dynamic range of their instrument in this setting. The listener senses that something is being held back, even when the music goes "all out."

Not only can an old piano sound uncannily like a violin or cello, it also lends itself to doubling. In Haydn's trios the cello parts double the left hand of the keyboard, just like the continuo line in a baroque ensemble. In that setting a cello and a harpsichord make an especially productive pair, since the harpsichord excels at articulating the beginning of the notes while the cello adds dynamic shaping and smoothness. In a fortepiano trio, even though the keyboard can shape the bass line on its own, the cello provides heft and color to balance the violin. But the modern piano's thick tenor and bass registers makes the cello's role nearly impossible to fulfill with any satisfaction, and Haydn's wonderful pieces have suffered unjustified neglect as a result.

Mozart and Beethoven recognized the possibility of freeing the cello from the responsibility of doubling the bass line; their trios feature much more independent cello parts than Haydn's. But the old conception of the accompanied keyboard sonata lived on: Schumann's piano quartet and quintet are filled with passages where the strings only reinforce a texture that is fully realized in the keyboard part alone. In my experience, string players love to play with period pianos—they finally feel like equal participants.

❧   ❧   ❧

Much of the classical repertory before Beethoven tends to be underappreciated today. Mark Twain famously said about Wagner that his music is "better than it sounds." Paraphrasing him, I hope to have persuaded you that much music by Mozart and Haydn is "better than it usually sounds," because critical features are often overlooked.

Chapter Four

Beethoven and the Evolving Piano

Beethoven speaks to us so directly that it's easy to ignore the distance separating our world from his. I want to re-situate him in his historical context, not as a prophetic genius ahead of his time, but as a practical musician whose compositions were conceived for performance by his contemporaries, for his contemporaries. First I will consider Beethoven's relationship with the pianos of his time, then examine how those instruments illuminate issues of tempo, articulation, voicing, and pedaling.

Pianos changed significantly during the first part of the nineteenth century: one obvious development was the growing range of the keyboard. At the beginning of Beethoven's career Mozart's five-octave range (FF–f^3) was still the norm, but the Erard that Beethoven acquired in 1803 had five-and-a-half octaves, FF–c^4. By 1810 a six-octave range (FF–f^4) was common, although by no means standard. Some makers offered a choice: through the 1820s Streicher and Graf made models with either six or six-and-a-half octaves (FF–f^4 or CC–f^4); g^4 is found on some Grafs from the late 1820s but does not appear on Streichers until the mid-1830s. (None of Mendelssohn's works requires the high G; Schumann uses it in a few pieces, including the C major Fantasy.) Many pianos of the 1850s had a seven-octave range, AAA–a^4 (eighty-five notes); our familiar eighty-eight only became standard at the end of the nineteenth century.

In another notable development after 1805, Viennese builders began to replace knee levers with actual pedals, following the example of the English. More and more pedals were added, peaking in the 1820s when some instruments had as many as seven, including percussion and other special effects. This trend was relatively short-lived; by the 1840s, the usual arrangement was two pedals, one to raise the dampers and the other to shift the keyboard (*una corda*).

There is further evidence that the Viennese were eyeing the products of their English competitors. Czerny said of Streicher that "by imitating English instruments, he was able to give his own [pianos] a fuller tone and a firmer mechanism than older pianofortes had had."[1] The larger, heavier instruments were generally louder than earlier ones, although it's worth noting that builders expended just as much effort on making them play quietly: the array of pedals might include *una corda* and *due corde* (causing the hammers to hit only one or two of the three strings), a single and a double moderator (putting one or two layers of cloth between hammer and strings), and a harp or *sourdine* stop (cloth or leather directly touching the strings to reduce their resonance).

Beethoven's Pianos

We have a pretty good idea of Mozart's taste in pianos; his praise for Stein's instruments in 1777 and his subsequent acquisition of a Walter by 1785 are well documented. So, if we use a Stein piano to play a piece Mozart wrote in 1778, or a Walter for one from 1785, our experience should correspond to his expectations. With Beethoven the situation could not be more different. Many instruments passed beneath his fingers, none of which seem to have pleased him completely. In 1796 he wrote to Andreas Streicher: "I received the day before yesterday your fortepiano, which is really an excellent instrument. Anybody else would try to keep it for himself . . . [but] it robs me of the freedom to create my own tone."[2]

It's difficult to interpret this statement, but Chopin used almost identical language to explain his preference for the Pleyel piano.[3] And in both cases, we are left to speculate whether today's Steinway might also have presented a "ready-made tone" that might satisfy "anyone else." But we do know that the Erard Beethoven acquired in 1803[4] didn't satisfy him either; he made repeated attempts to modify it, as testified by Streicher: "Beethoven is certainly a strong player, yet he is still unable to treat his [Erard] adequately, and he has already had it changed two times without the least improvement . . ."[5] The evidence suggests that Beethoven wanted the key dip shallower (i.e., more like a Viennese piano); further changes may have been necessary to compensate for the resulting increase in touch weight.[6]

In Part One of *Beethoven the Pianist*, Tilman Skowroneck lays out everything currently known about the specific pianos Beethoven played during his performing career. Here is a summary:

1. Beethoven's early training and his first successes were in Bonn, where, according to Junker, he was accustomed to playing only Stein's pianos.[7]

2. He arrived in Vienna in 1792 where he became acquainted with Walter pianos; by 1799 he had one in his home (this is attested to by Czerny, who was brought to Beethoven for lessons[8]). Compared to the Stein, the Walter would have been heavier and more suitable for virtuosic playing.

3. In 1803, Beethoven acquired an Erard piano with an English-style action, the range FF–c^4, and four pedals (*una corda*, moderator, lute-stop, and dampers). Although the piano was long thought to be a gift to Beethoven from the Erard firm, the recent discovery of an internal document in the Erard archives suggests that it was actually bought by the composer.[9] This purchase is in line with Beethoven's documented interest in the English piano style (he studied Clementi's works carefully and a copy of Cramer's études has been preserved with his personal annotations). 1803 is also the year in which Beethoven began to write pitches higher than g^3, but the relationship between the new piano and his use of the higher notes isn't direct. The "Waldstein" sonata was composed after the acquisition of the Erard, yet it only goes up to a^3, while the C minor concerto, written *before* he got the Erard, requires c^4. Commercial concerns may explain the more conservative range of the "Waldstein" sonata. Beethoven must have had access to a newer piano to perform the concerto, while the average purchaser of piano music would still have had an older instrument with the smaller range.[10]

4. By 1810 Beethoven called his Erard "simply not of any use any more, of none whatsoever."[11] And indeed, opus 81a, composed in 1809, already exceeds the Erard's range, reaching f^4.

Beethoven's last attempt at public performance, in 1811, was a disaster, presumably on account of his deafness. From then on, we find reports of his pianos in very poor condition, terribly out of tune and with broken strings. Nonetheless, he continued to respond to new developments in piano design. With opus 101 in 1816 he went below FF for the first time—writing "*contra E*" in the score to underline the novelty and the significance of the effect. Once again, Beethoven wasn't getting out in front of the builders; Streicher had already made instruments with CC–f^4 in 1807.

Other makers whose instruments have been associated with Beethoven are Broadwood and Graf. Much has been written about the piano that Beethoven received as a gift from the Broadwood company in 1818.[12] This instrument, at least with respect to its range of CC–c^4, must have seemed old-fashioned to the composer since he was already writing notes above c^4 in 1808. (Opus 110 and opus 111 may have been conceived on the Broadwood; those pieces both stay within its range.) But for opus 101 and the "Hammerklavier," both composed before the arrival of the Broadwood, he was most likely using a Streicher that he may have acquired in 1816.

In 1825 Conrad Graf loaned Beethoven a piano with four strings per note in the treble, fitted with a special stethoscope-like amplifying apparatus. Some writers presume that the quadruple stringing was an attempt by Graf to build an especially loud special piano for Beethoven, but there must be another explanation, since at least one other Graf survives with the same stringing. It seems more likely that the experimental design was judged unsuccessful (it would certainly have been difficult to keep in tune) and that Graf sent it to Beethoven because its defects would not be noticeable to the deaf composer. In any case Beethoven had already stopped writing for the piano by that time.

It is convenient and relevant to categorize these pianos by their range, but they were also designed to withstand increasing tension, with thicker strings and heavier hammers. These give the instruments a longer-sustaining sound, a darker tone color, and more power overall, although they still resemble Mozart's piano more than they do a modern grand. There was geographical diversity as well: the French Erard and English Broadwood represented quite different tonal styles from the prevailing Viennese aesthetic.

In sum, we cannot point to any instrument as "the Beethoven piano." Beethoven was intimately familiar with the wide range of instruments being produced during his lifetime, and although he certainly complained about them, he nevertheless wrote for them, adapting his style to their changing capabilities.

Was Beethoven Dreaming of the Modern Piano?

Did Renaissance artists dream of acrylic paints? Of course we have no way of knowing what they dreamt about, yet some version of this question lurks behind many modern attitudes to Beethoven and his piano music. It arises because of the following observations:

- Beethoven complained regularly about his pianos;
- Beethoven adopted newer pianos with their increased range throughout his career.

These two points taken together have been construed as "proof" that he would have preferred the modern piano, and that consequently we needn't trouble ourselves with the old ones. Even a thoughtful, historically aware performer like Robert Taub takes this notion for granted. Here he describes how he goes about learning a piece by Beethoven:

> I examine sketches and study autograph scores if available, read Beethoven's letters, *try to understand his frustrations with the pianofortes of his time* [emphasis mine], delve into the reasons for his often unconventional fingering and pedaling indications, and internalize all this so I can bring greater meaning to a performance, and come closer to the *Geist*—the spirit—of the music.[13]

If you look to an old piano only to find what Beethoven found frustrating, how will you discover any of the instrument's *positive* qualities?

We will never know what Beethoven would have thought of the modern piano, although he might not have liked it as much as we imagine: he apparently found the touch of his Erard too deep and too heavy, and the modern piano's action is even deeper and heavier. More importantly, we will never know what sort of music he might have composed for a modern piano, had he had one. But we do have the pieces he composed for the pianos he *did* know, and I am continually struck by how idiomatically he treated them. His special pedal effects, unlikely combinations of registers, and thickly voiced chords—often awkward or unconvincing on a modern piano—all demonstrate his absolute command of contemporary instruments. Amazingly, this is just as true of the late pieces, written for pianos that he only encountered after his hearing had deteriorated significantly.[14]

And let's not forget that Beethoven considered the pianos of his own time worthy of the lion's share of his compositional output. Beethoven would hardly have told his friends and colleagues, "I know my piano music sounds terrible today, but just wait a hundred years . . ." If he found the piano truly inadequate, he could have written more symphonic music and string quartets instead. In a later chapter Taub says: "I believe that Beethoven's works should be performed on the best possible instruments currently available, in a most sympathetic artistic manner. . . . If a concept of authenticity demands slavish adherence to period instruments exclusively, it becomes invalid."[15]

It's impossible to disagree with any of this. But the problematic word here is "best," since although a Steinway is "best" for filling a large hall with sound, it's not necessarily the "best" for communicating Beethoven's ideas about tempo, texture, articulation, or accent.

Charles Rosen is another brilliant performer-scholar who dismisses the relevance of Beethoven's pianos for today's players. He hints at his complicated attitude towards historical instruments in the early pages of two of his books. He chose to play the musical illustrations that accompany *Beethoven's Piano Sonatas: A Short Companion* on an 1879 Bechstein "that Liszt had admired, and of which the sounding-board still produced a lovely tone with a remarkably long decay of sound that every piano ideally should have. The sonority was closer to a piano of 1810 than most modern pianos . . ."[16] If "closer to a piano of 1810" was desired, why settle for 1879? And a "remarkably long decay" is not always a virtue, as I show throughout this book.

Rosen's *The Romantic Generation* begins by describing a musical passage that depends on the listener hearing a sound that is not present. Just like Taub, Rosen focuses on what an instrument *cannot* do, rather than on what it does:[17]

> At the climax of the final movement of the Sonata in C minor, op. 111, by Beethoven, most pianists take (correctly, I think) so slow a tempo that the culminating B♭ has died away long before it is resolved . . . On one of Beethoven's pianos the B♭ decays very quickly, and even on a modern concert grand it has diminished to inaudibility before its resolution to an A♮ . . . More than any composer before him, Beethoven understood the pathos of the gap between idea and realization, and the sense of strain put on the listener's imagination is essential here. The best argument for using the pianos of Beethoven's time in place of the modern grand piano is not the aptness of the old instruments but their greater inadequacy for realizing such an effect, and consequently the more dramatic effort required of the listener. The modern piano, however, is sufficiently inadequate to convey Beethoven's intentions.

Although the modern piano may be "sufficiently inadequate" to sustain the bb^3 referenced in the quote (mm. 118–19 of the second movement of opus 111), it alters many other passages in ways that Rosen chooses to disregard. Most of the time, Beethoven asks for effects that were perfectly realizable on the pianos of his time, and—with care and some adjustments—on modern ones as well.

But I would be remiss if I didn't point out a circumstance that appears to support Mr. Taub's and Mr. Rosen's position. The B-flat concerto, opus 19, was published in 1801, and in 1809 Beethoven composed a new cadenza for it, probably for a performance by his pupil the Archduke Rudolph. This cadenza, a monumental contrapuntal masterwork in Beethoven's mature style (closer to the "Emperor" concerto than to op. 19), is unplayable on the Mozartean five-octave piano for which the concerto was conceived; evidently an "up-to-date" piano with a six-octave range was used for this performance. If Beethoven didn't think a five-octave piano was needed for a performance of opus 19, why should we? After all, it would have been easier for him to find one in 1809 than it is for most of us today.

One answer is that the six-octave piano of 1809 was not all that different from the earlier five-octave piano. They certainly resemble each other far more than either resembles the modern Steinway. But there is a more fundamental answer: we need the old piano for reasons that did not concern Beethoven. Unlike him, we are grappling with music that was written in a different age, for a different world. Just because it has become very familiar to us does not mean that we understand it fully. We want all the help we can get, taking advantage of every clue that might bring us closer to the spirit behind the works; Beethoven himself had no such need.

Elements of Performance

Tempo Choice

The only piano piece for which Beethoven provided metronome markings is the "Hammerklavier" sonata—and his tempo for the first movement is so fast that no recording even comes close.[18] But Czerny's *On the Proper Performance of all of Beethoven's Works for the Piano* proposes viable metronome indication for every movement, along with other observations and advice. This volume belongs on every pianist's shelf, not just because the hints are useful, but because of the long and close relationship between the two men. Czerny was brought to Beethoven for lessons in 1801, when he was ten years old, and they remained on friendly terms until Beethoven's death. With this book Czerny attempted to preserve and transmit the legacy of his friend and former teacher; reading it now is like having a lesson with Czerny in 1842.[19] The metronome indications, plus another set supplied by Czerny for the Simrock edition (not always in agreement!) and those of Ignaz Moscheles (another important friend of Beethoven and advocate for his music), are reprinted in Appendix B of Rosenblum.[20]

As we have seen previously (Chapter 2, p. 16; Mozart K. 282 case study, p. 53), the modern piano not only permits but actively encourages slower tempi than are possible on the older ones. When playing slowly, we attend to the decay of the individual sounds. The longer they resonate, the longer we wait before playing the next note, and the slower the tempo. Unsurprisingly, the biggest difference is found in the slowest movements, such as the *Largo e mesto* from the D major sonata, op. 10, no. 3. The slow, stately pace of a (beautiful) performance like Alfred Brendel's (♪=ca. 46) is impossible to sustain on the fortepiano. With a faster basic tempo (Czerny suggests ♪=72) the player can group the notes into larger gestures separated by breaths.

Sensitive players encountering a historical piano for the first time will instinctively speed up the tempo of slow pieces, which may lead to other adjustments, as reported by this student who worked on opus 109 at the Graf: "I had to increase the tempo of the slow music (*adagio espressivo* sections of the first movement; the theme and variations 1, 2, 4, 6 of the third), since the sounds die away so soon after the initial attack. The faster tempo allowed for a smoother and more singing style of phrasing, as well as greater rhythmic flexibility."

One might imagine that the quicker tempo, with its "more singing style of phrasing, as well as greater rhythmic flexibility," could be transferred directly to the modern piano, but when the slower-developing tones don't have time to bloom, the music sounds agitated and rushed. The historical piano and a quicker tempo foster greater flexibility and can help students find a "more singing style," but in order to project the same atmosphere at the modern piano, it's often necessary to play more slowly. But not *too* slowly!

Here is another student, describing a similar experience with the slow movement of the Fourth Concerto:

> At the modern piano, one may be tempted to play the passage very slowly. Although it can be very convincing, this interpretation completely distorts the character communicated by the tempo dictated by the forepiano. A more moving tempo gives the phrase more unity and allows it to breathe. It's perfectly possible to do this on a modern piano. You just have to lighten the texture of the chords by voicing the outer voices, and listen for the long phrase.

Note the crucial role of *character* in the student's argument. He doesn't advocate playing faster at the modern piano because the *tempo* is more authentic, but rather because his experience at the fortepiano revealed a *character* that he found more authentic. Communicating that character at the modern piano involved adjustments beyond changing the tempo.

To test the theory that the modern piano leads pianists to adopt a slow tempo, I sampled as many recordings of the Fourth Concerto as I could find. In many of the modern-piano performances, the orchestra begins at a moderate speed—not far from the 84 recommended by Czerny—and then the piano enters much more slowly, often close to 60 (typical were Hélène Grimaud with Kurt Masur, or Leon Fleisher with George Szell). Of the three fortepiano performances I examined—Steven Lubin (with Christopher Hogwood), Robert Levin (with John Eliot Gardiner), and Melvyn Tan (with Roger Norrington)—even the slowest (Levin/Gardiner) is considerably faster than most modern pianists. However, András Schiff (with Bernard Haitink), on a modern instrument, plays almost as quickly as the fastest of the fortepiano versions (Tan/Norrington). Schiff has performed on period pianos, which may have influenced his tempo choice, or perhaps it's just a coincidence.

Tempo Flexibility

Regardless of the tempo, old recordings and accounts of Beethoven's own playing suggest a much freer attitude to time than we generally encounter today. Here is a note made by Beethoven on the score of the song *Nord oder Süd*, composed in 1817: "100 according to Maelzel; but this must be held applicable to only the first measures, for feeling also has its tempo and this cannot entirely be expressed in this figure."[21]

The most detailed descriptions of Beethoven's attitude towards tempo flexibility come from his friend Anton Schindler. Unfortunately, Schindler's reliability is questionable: he is known to have forged entries in Beethoven's conversation books, presumably to inflate his connection to Beethoven. But his reports are vivid and illuminating, even if they were exaggerated.

> All the pieces which I have heard Beethoven himself play were, with few exceptions, given without any constraint as to the rate of the time. He adopted a *tempo-rubato* in the proper sense of the term, according as subject and situation might demand, without the slightest approach to caricature. Beethoven's playing was the most *distinct* and *intelligible declamation* . . .

And later:

> Beethoven himself said that the pace of this rich movement (op. 10 no. 3, mvt. 2) must be changed fully ten times, though only so as to be perceptible to the most sensitive ear. The principal theme is always to be repeated in the tempo of

its first statement; all the rest is subject to variation in the tempo, each phrase according to its own meaning.[22]

A more reliable observer, Beethoven's pupil Ferdinand Ries, wrote: "in general, [he] played his own compositions very much according to his humor, though he usually kept a very steady rhythm and only occasionally, indeed, very rarely, speeded up the tempo somewhat. At times he restrained the tempo in his crescendo with a ritardando, which had a beautiful and most striking effect."[23]

Perhaps these contradictions are to be expected, since *rubato* is subtle, and any description will reflect the taste of the listener. After all, even Ries, who felt that Beethoven "*usually* kept a very steady rhythm," noted that "*at times*" he combined crescendo with ritardando, and occasionally accelerated the tempo.

Czerny, besides his prescribed metronome indications, frequently admonishes the player not to modify the tempo, especially in slow movements. Here is what he says about the first three sonatas: For op. 2, no. 1, "Here [in the *Adagio* movement], a refined touch, a perfect *legato*, and a strict preservation of the time, are especially effective." For op. 2, no. 2, "The whole [of the *Largo* movement] in strict time, but the conclusion *ritardando*." And for op. 2, no. 3, "The beginning of this *Adagio* must be played with great sentiment, but strictly in time . . ."[24] In *The Pianist as Orator,* George Barth describes the transformation of musical style from a rhetorical one modeled on speech, with relatively free declamation and tempo modification, to the metronome-influenced style familiar to us today. According to him, this change had already begun in the first part of the nineteenth century, with Czerny among the modernizers, Schindler upholding the old style, and Beethoven himself as a pivotal figure, maintaining aspects of the old while blazing new trails.

Early recordings give us direct access to performance styles very distant from our own. There are none by Beethoven or his contemporaries, of course. But the oldest ones document the practices of musicians who grew up in the middle of the nineteenth century and were certainly much closer to Beethoven than we are. Robert Philip analyzed many recordings from the period 1900–1950, and found that tempo variation within a movement was greatest in the early years of the twentieth century, and has steadily decreased.[25] His examples include Beethoven's Violin Concerto and the "Kreutzer" sonata. In both of these works, the oldest performers speed up for the lively music and slow down for the lyrical themes, while the newer recordings show a gradual tendency towards uniformity of tempo.

Finally, we might consider the role that improvisation played in Beethoven's musical practice. This quote, from a letter by Camille Pleyel, is typical: "he gave me much pleasure when improvising. He does not improvise coldly like Woelfl. He realizes whatever enters his head and he is extremely daring. Sometimes he does astonishing things."[26] This tells us nothing at all about how Beethoven would have performed (or would have wanted *us* to perform) his published works, and doesn't even reveal much about how he improvised. But it does suggest that the sort of metronomically accurate performances we often hear today might have struck Pleyel as more like Woelfl's style than Beethoven's.

We have already seen how historical instruments encourage a quicker tempo in slow music, and that the increase in speed promotes greater rhythmic flexibility. But, in my experience, the old instruments seem to inspire freer declamation even without changing the tempo. What accounts for that? And can those instruments help us recover the freedom heard on early twentieth-century recordings?

Once again, I find myself comparing pianos and vehicles. Fortepianos are like sports cars or jet skis that are designed to start or stop abruptly and to take sharp curves at high speed. All have very little inertia, and react quickly to sudden changes in input. Because they cater to their operator's impulses, their strong suit is improvisation, not cruise control; they are better for delivering thrills and shocks than a smooth ride. But modern instruments can also be played in an improvisatory way. Listening to old recordings, experimenting with tempo flexibility, actually improvising at the piano—all these can free us up, and bring us closer to Beethoven's style.

Articulation

Beethoven's approach to articulation should be seen in the context of two broad trends, both related to the gradual replacement of the harpsichord by the fortepiano:

- an increasing preference for legato as the prevailing, "default" touch;
- an increased reliance on dynamic effects, including accents, to organize the musical material.

The shift towards legato is documented in many treatises from the early nineteenth century,[27] and the rising importance of dynamics may be largely related to the abandonment of the harpsichord (although we may wonder which was the chicken, which the egg). In his memoirs, Czerny both describes and situates Beethoven's use of legato: "making me particularly aware of the Legato of which he had such an unrivalled command, and which all other pianists at that time considered unfeasible at the pianoforte; choppy and smartly detached playing [*das gehackte und kurz gestossene Spiel*] was still in favour then . . ."[28]

Beethoven's quest for a legato style may also explain his interest in English-style pianos (including his 1803 Erard) and English pianists such as Clementi and Cramer. As Kalkbrenner wrote in his treatise in 1831: "The English pianos . . . have caused the professional musicians of that country to adopt a grander style and that beautiful way of singing which distinguishes them . . ."[29] Because Beethoven's legato playing was praised by his contemporaries, today's pianists may be forgiven for presuming that our current practices—also notable for their emphasis on legato—are entirely appropriate for Beethoven or, indeed, that they actually originated with him. This section will show how Beethoven's works still depend on the kind of inflection that characterized the style of the previous generation.

The new elements are easy to see, especially the longer slurs. But the modern way of playing, with its nearly continuous legato, seems equally at odds with the details that we find in Beethoven's scores. After all, none of the pianos of Beethoven's time (neither the Viennese nor the English) had anything like the slow-developing tone and long sustain of the modern piano. Instead, their quicker decay encouraged the subtle, expressive use of articulation between notes, while their shallow key dip made those details relatively easy to execute and control. Beethoven took full advantage of these qualities. His music is filled with marks relating to articulation: slurs of every possible length, dots, wedges, and combinations of slurs with dots or wedges. The signs for emphasis (*sf*, *fz*, *fp*, >), although they refer principally to dynamics, often have implications for articulation as well. The sheer quantity and variety of these directions attest to their importance to Beethoven, but their meaning is not always obvious. This section will focus on the slurs: where they end, how they divide phrases into segments, and where they appear to be missing altogether.

Do I have to?
All too often, faced with instructions that seem odd or confusing, even well-intentioned musicians just ignore the markings in favor of what sounds "musical." Of course no one should *ever* play something just because "it's written that way." If the music doesn't make sense to the performer it surely won't make sense to the listener! But the better we understand Beethoven's intentions, the more sympathy we may have for his demands.

Outside of music, "to slur" is defined as "to render confused or indistinct; to blur"; *slurred speech* is characteristic of a drunk person. Its opposite is *articulate* speech, meaning "consisting of clearly distinguishable parts." The classical style is almost always articulate, the component parts clearly distinguishable; that is one of its defining qualities. In eighteenth-century musical practice, articulation served what could be considered a *grammatical* function: it was expected or required in various contexts, just as capital letters or commas are necessary in written English. Upbeats were almost universally separated from downbeats, appoggiaturas and syncopes were preceded by an articulation, and resolutions on downbeats ("masculine endings") were also articulated. So were harmony changes and important events of all kinds. These conventions seemed to be dissolving at the end of the century; in his later pieces even Mozart sometimes broke the rules.

Beethoven used slurs in new ways, often covering features that would have required articulation in the old style, in other places interrupting slurs unexpectedly in mid-phrase. Anthony Pay's theory that every slurred group represents the ornamentation of a single pitch does not always apply to Beethoven, whose indications are sometimes totally independent of grouping or structure. Freed of their grammatical function, slurs became performance directions linked to *expression*. Harnoncourt's belief that music after 1800 *paints* instead of *speaking* points to this new willingness to break the bonds between music and speech. The new style of articulation blurs the boundaries between individual musical components in the interest of a broader picture.

The following examples are designed:

- to convince you that Beethoven's slurs, even when puzzling, are still meaningful (although you may not need any persuading on this point);

- to show how the classical understanding of articulation is still relevant to Beethoven's music;
- to identify Beethoven's innovative uses of articulation;
- to suggest ways to perform these details convincingly on any piano.

Example 4.1 begins with four short slurs followed by a longer one. Evidently Beethoven had something in mind that would not be communicated by a single continuous slur.[30] But how should the phrase be performed?

One could play measure 1 (and m. 3) crescendo to create two-measure swells, but I prefer to follow eighteenth-century practice and play the first measure diminuendo. This gives the second measure the same shape as the first, but intensified by the higher register, the *sf*, and the addition of a third voice. After four repetitions of this short, one-measure shape the long slur creates an even more satisfying contrast, and I find actual spaces between the slurs just as effective on the modern piano as on the fortepiano. Four bars later Beethoven develops this idea, this time contradicting the normal shape of the long slur with a hairpin (engraved under the left hand because there's no other place for it), and further emphasizing the end of the phrase by ending the slur early.

The Henle edition silently "corrects" Beethoven's text by extending both the slur and the hairpin through the fourth bar; the Associated Board's version uses a dotted line to extend the slur, with a suggestion in the accompanying commentary that the crescendo might also be extended. Since the

Example 4.1. Beethoven, Sonata no. 2 in A major, op. 2, no. 2, mvt. 3, mm. 45–62.

first edition (Artaria's from 1796) is the only authentic source for this piece, the editors in both cases must have felt that these last three notes (d^1–c^1–b) could only have been detached by mistake. I believe it was a conscious choice on Beethoven's part, adding to the intensity at the end of the crescendo.

Opus 7 uses a similar strategy (Example 4.2). I would be sure to give the two-measure slurs in measures 5–6 and 7–8 the traditional diminuendo shape, maximizing the impact of the subsequent longer slurs with their special dynamic effects. I have reproduced measures 13–20 from the original edition (Example 4.3) to show how difficult it was for the engraver to snake the slurs between the voices—a detail that must have been very important to Beethoven!

Finally, the contrasting indications for the two hands in passages like the one shown in Example 4.4 only make sense if Beethoven expected articulation between successive slurs.

The previous examples showed how Beethoven uses slurs of varying sizes to underline the structure; the next ones concern the slur+1 pattern discussed in Chapter 3. Beethoven seems to have been particularly interested in this figure, referring to it in a letter to the violinist Karl Holz, who was preparing the opus 132 quartet for publication: "For God's sake please impress on Rampl [the copyist] to copy everything exactly as it stands . . . The slurs should be exactly as they are now. It is not at all the same whether it is like this or like this."[31] Example 4.5 reproduces the notation from the letter.

Example 4.2. Beethoven, Sonata no. 4 in E-flat major, op. 7, mvt. 1, mm. 1–13.

Example 4.3. Beethoven, Sonata no. 4 in E-flat major, op. 7, mvt. 1, mm. 13–20 (first edition, Artaria, 1797).

Example 4.4. Beethoven, Sonata no. 4 in E-flat major, op. 7, mvt. 1, mm. 21–24.

Example 4.5. Beethoven, letter to Karl Holz, August 15, 1825.

In op. 10, no. 2 (written long before opus 132), Beethoven exploits both versions (Example 4.6). He begins with two chords—an eighth-note upbeat and a downbeat—then transforms that idea by replacing the first chord with a triplet (circled). With classical-style articulation between the triplet and the downbeat we can still hear the two distinct items, rather than a single four-note shape. The long slur that follows is very different; even the upbeat is slurred—very unclassically—to the rest of the phrase. At measures 16–18 Beethoven drives home his point: the original rhythmic figure is transformed by the four-note slur (also circled).

The challenge for the player is to make the distinction clearly audible. It's easier at the fortepiano; on the modern piano I finger the initial triplet 2–1–3–1.

Example 4.6. Beethoven, Sonata no. 6 in F major, op. 10, no. 2, mvt. 1, mm. 1–20.

Here is an exercise for practicing slur +1. In Example 4.7 below first use my suggested fingering, playing the third and fourth notes with the same finger to guarantee a clear articulation. Then, try to match the result with a more usual fingering.

Example 4.7. Beethoven, Sonata no. 3 in C major, op. 10, no. 3, mvt. 3, mm. 1–2.

Since there are no autographs for any of these early sonatas, we have to presume that the first editions reliably transmit Beethoven's intentions. Fortunately the slurs seem very carefully engraved, and it is worth comparing these examples with another early sonata, op. 2, no. 2 (Example 4.8):

Example 4.8. Beethoven, Sonata no. 2 in A major, op. 2, no. 2, mvt. 1, mm. 1–4, 76–79.

This time, there is a slur over the barline right at the beginning of the piece, and the association of slurred speech with drunkenness seems particularly appropriate here. (Does this motive portray someone with hiccups? or falling down?) But at measure 76, when the music has become much more serious and vehement, the figure acquires the more formal, "classical" articulation. The slurred, *p* version never recurs; from here on, the final note of the figure is always articulated, and the motive is always *f* or *ff*.

I've chosen two more examples to show how Beethoven uses small changes of articulation to develop his materials. Example 4.9 is the slow movement of opus 7:

Example 4.9. Beethoven, Sonata no. 4 in E-flat major, op. 7, mvt. 2, mm. 1–4.

Compare measure 4 with measure 2. While the left hand provides a sonorous, legato underpinning (it's especially easy to slide the thumb from F♯ to F on the fortepiano), Beethoven asks for an articulation in the right hand, reinforced by *sf*. To guarantee a clear attack in all the voices, I release both A and D simultaneously before the chord; of course this detail is lost if the pedal is used to cover the gap.

Example 4.10 is from the third movement of the same sonata.

Example 4.10. Beethoven, Sonata no. 4 in E-flat major, op. 7, mvt. 3, mm. 1–6, 15–19.

Consider the articulation between measures 3 and 4. As in the previous example, another voice, this time the tenor, covers the space in the upper part. Bringing out this articulation clarifies two features of Beethoven's design: the immediate repetition of measure 4's gesture in measures 5 and 6, and the subsequent reinterpretation of this motive in measures 15–19. What had been separate is now joined; what had been joined is now separated, and the changes are reinforced by *staccato* and *sf.*

The irregular slurs in the next set of examples interrupt long melodic lines at points that do not always coincide with the natural syntax of the pitches. Notably, each movement's performance directions refer explicitly to a singing style: "*Adagio cantabile*" for the "Pathétique," "*sehr singbar vorgetragen*" for the second movement of opus 90, "*molto cantabile*" for the theme of the last movement of opus 109. These slurs are problematic if our model for singing is the continuous legato of Italian *bel canto*. But the articulations that Beethoven prescribes—carried out subtly and sympathetically—are perfectly compatible with the natural declamation of consonant-heavy German words.

William Newman seems to find the slurring of the slow movement of the "Pathétique" particularly exasperating. He devotes two pages to this passage (see Example 4.11), first considering and then discarding the idea that Beethoven used slurs "to mask square syntax." As he puts it, "the bulk of the evidence—early, middle, and late—contradicts [this] suggestion . . . for his slurs more often do coincide with the straightforward syntax that prevails in his themes . . ."[32]

If we regard the slurs purely as performance instructions, not "phrasing," the problem vanishes completely. The first four bars include two moves from c^1 to eb^1 (indicated with arrows), and Beethoven shows us how to interpret them. The initial slur serves to "downgrade" the first eb^1 while the articulation

Example 4.11. Beethoven, Sonata no. 8 in C minor, "Pathetique," op. 13, mvt. 2, mm. 1–8.

between measures 3 and 4 emphasizes the more important E♭ of measure 4, supported by the arrival on the dominant. The next slur (e♭¹–e♮¹–f¹) makes no sense grammatically, but, executed with a diminuendo according to the rules, produces a tender performance of the f¹ (circled); the break between f¹ and the following b♭ brings out the unexpected drop in register.

When the text seems confusing, editors are tempted to make adjustments in favor of consistency or clarity. But to a performer, details of declamation that convey variety, surprise, and even ambiguity can be virtues, and Beethoven's pianos were well-suited to deliver them. With a smoother surface we may enhance our "atmosphere-painting," but not without giving up some "speaking."

The second movement of opus 90 (Example 4.12) features especially un-classical articulation: Mozart might have separated the sixteenth-note upbeats from the downbeat of measure 1, the double appoggiaturas at the beginning of measure 2 from the preceding notes, and the arrival of the tonic in measure 4 from the dominant harmony at the end of measure 3. Yet this is far from a continuous legato: most of the slurs cover six notes or fewer, and they are interspersed with notes marked *portato* or even *staccato*.

At the beginning of the third movement of opus 109 (Example 4.13), Beethoven staggers the slur lengths in the two hands, minimizing the moments when the entire texture breathes. This allows him to present a highly articulated melody without dryness (as long as the efforts of the pianist's right hand aren't undone by the pedaling).

The next three examples concern the distinction between legato and "ordinary touch." This was discussed in the previous chapter, and although the evidence suggests a growing preference for legato in the early nineteenth century, ordinary touch didn't simply disappear. In these examples Beethoven appears to be juxtaposing the two styles. Judge for yourself whether he simply forgot to mark the slurs. (And be careful with the editions you use: some

Example 4.12. Beethoven, Sonata no. 27 in E minor, op. 90, mvt. 2, mm. 1–4.

Example 4.13. Beethoven, Sonata no. 30 in E major, op. 109, mvt. 3, mm. 1–8.

Example 4.14. Beethoven, Sonata no. 7 in D major, op. 10, no. 3, mvt. 4, mm. 106–13.

editors supply all the "missing" slurs, and even when they put them within parentheses, those parentheses are easy to overlook . . .)

In Example 4.14, the contrast between legato for the scales and non-legato for the arpeggios seems intentional to me; a lightly articulated touch adds sparkle to the final bars.

Throughout the last movement of opus 26 (Example 4.15) the sixteenth notes are never slurred when they accompany the eighth-note legato melody (i.e., m. 3 in the right hand or m. 9 in the left hand). I use overholding to make the slurred passages as different as possible from the non-legato ones.

At the beginning of opus 79 we find a further distinction: four bars of slurred eighth notes are followed by four bars of unmarked ("ordinary") eighths, after which Beethoven writes *leggiermente* ("lightly"—usually defined as a light, semi-staccato), another step farther from legato.

These examples all accord with Charles Rosen's assessment: "Beethoven does not use the old-fashioned, detached or non-legato technique of playing for its own sake for long stretches, but only in order to achieve a more interesting variety of textures. The detached sonority is generally followed at once by another kind of touch."[33]

Beethoven demands more legato than many earlier composers, but he is still working with the classical language; a continuous, smooth line that disregards his careful directions is as inappropriate here as it would be for Mozart. That disregard can already be seen in the generations immediately after Beethoven, as George Barth has shown.[34] Czerny was proud that he knew all of Beethoven's works from memory, but his version of the opening

Example 4.15. Beethoven, Sonata no. 12 in A-flat major, op. 26, mvt. 4, mm. 1–10.

Example 4.16. Beethoven, Sonata no. 12 in A-flat major, op. 26, mvt. 1, mm. 1–8 (from Czerny, *On the Proper Performance*, p. 47)

of opus 26 (Example 4.16) omits the carefully notated slurs and dots of the original edition (shown in Example 2.5, p. 18).

It was in connection with this very sonata that I first used the term *pronunciation* to speak about slurs. I wanted a student to play less like Czerny's version and more like Beethoven's, but the results were discouraging. The more he focused on articulation, the choppier and less satisfying his playing became. When, instead, I asked him to *clearly pronounce* the first note of each new slur—as though saying a word that began with a consonant—the improvement was dramatic. The student felt that he was playing a longer line, and I got the "speaking" quality that I was looking for. This led me to the following formulation: Beethoven's style must have been noticeably smoother than Mozart's, but he was no less concerned with how the music is to be *pronounced*.

Here are some suggestions for putting these ideas into practice:

1. Read the music very carefully. Notice the smallest variations in the notation; good composers take pains to show us what they want.

2. *Sing!* We are much more natural musicians when we sing—even if the pitches are nearly unrecognizable. Notice the syllables you choose (pah–pah–pah, ta–dah, etc.), and pay special attention to the consonants (p, b, t, d, l . . .). Those are your articulations. Make sure you still recognize them when you play; that's how to make your music speak.

3. Try playing without pedal. Many pianists have an unconscious tendency to fill in every space, creating long lines without breaths even in the earliest stages of learning the music. *Listen* to the way one slur relates to the next.

4. Try to shape slurs with diminuendo—or, at least without crescendo. Structuring every gesture as a crescendo towards a goal—a typical strategy in Romantic music—is less appropriate in earlier styles.
5. Experiment with fingerings that force you to articulate. (You don't have to use them in performance . . .)

Texture: Chords

Even Beethoven's earliest music *sounds* very different from Mozart or Haydn, and the differences are, if anything, more apparent at the fortepiano. Thicker chords, more active accompaniments, wider arpeggios, and unusual pedal effects make the five-octave instrument seem bigger than it does in earlier repertoire. Because these techniques are also well-suited to the modern piano, Beethoven appears more idiomatically pianistic to us than earlier composers. But the modern piano's lush, full sound can also be a disadvantage in his music, especially where Beethoven writes closely spaced chords, as in Example 4.17. On the fortepiano this passage sounds like a brass choir, each voice round and distinct, but at the modern piano the chords are unclear unless the top line is voiced strongly.

Example 4.18 is more typical. Here the open spacing of the chords and their placement in the middle register produces a clearer texture, but playing the voices equally on a modern piano still produces an unfocused and amateurish sound compared to the singing quality that results from well-defined voicing.

At the fortepiano the effect is exactly the opposite. Favoring the top voice makes the fortepiano sound thin, while the equal-voiced version sounds vibrant and full. That version produced a striking insight: with all four voices present, the opening suggests a chorale. In conjunction with Beethoven's careful dating of the autograph—December 25, 1821—are we meant to

Example 4.17. Beethoven, Sonata no. 23 in F minor, "Appassionata," op. 57, mvt. 2, mm. 1–8.

Example 4.18. Beethoven, Sonata no. 31 in A-flat major, op. 110, mvt. 1, mm. 1–4.

Example 4.19. Beethoven, Sonata no. 31 in A-flat major, op. 110, mvt. 3, mm. 9–12.

consider this piece in a religious light? If you agree, then you could evoke the sound of a choir, even on a modern piano: start with a clear image of all the voices, and create the fullest possible texture while still maintaining a focused sound. Shallow pedaling often helps; clear articulation in every voice is a must.

The *Arioso* section of this sonata (Example 4.19) also presents a challenging texture. On a modern piano the melody sounds most beautiful when the left hand is minimized, yet the gravity and pathos of the passage are conveyed primarily by the chords. A fortepiano player has little choice here: the chords *must* carry the music forward, since the right hand's notes do not sustain very long. Because Beethoven's conception depends on both components, I recommend practicing with the left hand alone, and only adding the melody when as much expression as possible has been wrung from the accompaniment.

Texture and the Illusion of Space

We often use spatial metaphors to describe musical phenomena. For example, a passage played softly can suggest that the music is taking place at a distance, while crescendo and diminuendo can create the impression of music approaching or receding. Similarly, a melody played loudly appears in the foreground; a quieter accompaniment seems situated somewhere "behind" the soloist. This effect is most obvious when the functions of melody and accompaniment are divided between two instruments, as in the F major cello sonata shown in Example 4.20. On Beethoven's piano, the repeated chords in both hands (mm. 49–52) provide an insistent, lively motor; the instrument's transparency allows the cello to be heard clearly. The thicker sound of the modern piano risks drowning out the melody, but underplaying the piano part can reduce it to a distant strumming.

The same considerations apply when the piano plays the theme (mm. 35–38). The inherent balance between the registers of the fortepiano tolerates a very active left hand; to achieve this effect on the modern piano, strive for the "sweet spot" that provides an appropriate balance between the hands without

Example 4.20. Beethoven, Sonata for Piano and Violoncello in F major, op. 5, no. 1, mvt. 2, mm. 35–38, 49–52.

relegating the rhythmic element completely to the background. It isn't easy! I start with little or no pedal, lean a bit more on the thumb's voice than on the bass, and try to maintain a gentle pulsation on each group of four.

Pedal

Many pianists recognize that their usual mode of pedaling may not be appropriate for Bach, Haydn, or Mozart. But with Beethoven, they believe, "historical" concerns no longer apply, and one need only respond "artistically," as Robert Taub put it (quoted on p. 69). Another line of reasoning: Beethoven's contemporaries observed that Beethoven used the pedal "a lot,"[35] and so do today's pianists. Does that mean he pedaled just as we do? I doubt it, and not just because he played very different pianos from ours. To understand Beethoven, we need to remember that he studied with Haydn and he heard Mozart play. That was his point of departure. He never knew a note of Chopin.

What is *our* point of departure? It is, generally, the sound of a modern piano with the pedal continually depressed. Joseph Banowetz makes the point clearly, near the beginning of his book on pedaling: "The pedal's role in enriching the tone quality by permitting the activation of a rich conflicting mixture of sympathetic partials is of the greatest importance. It is not too extreme to regard this role as equivalent to the vibrato of the singer or the string player."[36]

But we now know that the modern style of near-continuous vibrato in singing and string playing was not practiced in the classical period, and, according to the evidence, nor was continuous pedaling.

So How Did *Beethoven Pedal?*

The role of the pedal seems to have changed definitively sometime after 1790. The earliest printed pedal markings appeared in Paris in the early 1790s, in the works of Daniel Steibelt and François-Adrien Boieldieu. Haydn's "open pedal" indications in the C major sonata from 1794 (Example 3.38, p. 62) resemble similar instructions in contemporary pieces by Cramer and Clementi. Example 4.21 shows Beethoven's first reference to the pedal, in a sketch dated sometime between 1790 and 1792. As we can see from his indication "mit dem knie" ("with the knee"), there was still no accepted notation for the pedal; Beethoven did not include pedal indications in his works until the publication of opus 26 in 1801, where the words *senza sordini* ("without

Example 4.21. Beethoven, "Kafka" sketchbook, folio 96r.

mutes") mean "raise the dampers" and *con sordini* ("with mutes") cancels the instruction.

It remains difficult to determine how Beethoven used the pedal, even after the appearance of these markings. Many pieces have no indications at all; some have only a few. In opus 28 *senza sordino/con sordino* appears only once (Example 4.22) but this cannot be the only spot for pedal in the entire sonata. Rather, Beethoven indicated pedaling only for unusual effects such as pedaling through rests or through harmony changes, or because he wants the pedal to be released at a particular point.[37] Here I think he wants the pedal maintained until the music resumes after the fermata, without a break or breath. He uses the pedal in a similar way to connect movements, for example at the end of the first movement of opus 109.

Of course, this raises the question: What sort of pedaling *was* usual for Beethoven or his contemporaries? Could it have been the same as for Banowetz, writing in 1985? This is unlikely, since the past 200 years have seen changes in musical style, instruments, and taste that surely affected pedaling as well. My proposals draw on three sources: first, hands-on experience with period instruments; secondly, treatises—most helpfully, Hummel's *Anweisung*; and finally, a comprehensive look at all of Beethoven's

Example 4.22. Beethoven, Sonata no. 15 in D major, op. 28, mvt. 1, mm. 250–56 (pedal markings as in the first edition).

indications—since, although they are far less common than we might like, at least they reveal what he thought required notating.

Evidence from Instruments

I have already suggested that the first generation of Viennese pianists routinely played without pedal, reserving it for special effects (C. P. E. Bach's "undamped register"). One factor was the coexistence of the piano with other keyboard instruments that had no pedal; another was the basic sound of the fortepiano, relatively rich in upper partials compared to the modern piano. Practical experience also confirms that eighteenth-century Viennese pianos are comfortable to play with little or no pedal. But their quicker decay and greater clarity also permit longer pedals than today's instruments.

The situation in England was different. English pianos had actual pedals long before the Viennese builders adopted them, and English composers began putting pedal indications in their scores well before their Viennese counterparts. Just as the precise damping and bright sound of Viennese pianos encourage light, detached playing, the darker sound and relatively hazy damping of the English pianos encourage *cantabile* playing with heavy use of the pedal. Composers of the English school seemed particularly attracted to the dreamy sound of long-held pedals; we have already seen Haydn's borrowing of this technique in the C major sonata composed while he was in London. Beethoven was also drawn to similar effects, as in Example 4.23, or in the last movement of the "Waldstein" (to be discussed further, below).

The combination of these two factors—the possibility of playing with no pedal at all, and the attractiveness of strikingly long pedals—allowed Beethoven to use the contrast between "dry" and "wet" passages for structural purposes. Unfortunately, modern instruments discourage this contrast. We rarely play the "normal" passages without any pedal because they sound too dry on our instruments, while the modern piano's long resonance makes

Example 4.23. Beethoven, Sonata no. 28 in A major, op. 101, mvt. 2, mm. 30–34.

the "English-style" passages too messy. Furthermore, blurring the harmony by means of the pedal is now considered "impressionistic," so today's players strive to play those passages more cleanly, even though such effects were clearly notated by Haydn, Beethoven, Clementi, and others.

Evidence from Treatises

C. P. E. Bach mentions the piano's "undamped register" briefly in his 1753 publication, but in 1797 Johann Peter Milchmeyer devoted an entire chapter of his treatise to "Mutations," his term for the various pedals that began appearing on pianos of his day. Their importance to him can be seen from the following quote:

> If you have a choice among various kinds of instruments, I suggest the small square piano. The big one needs more space, increases the cost of transport when travelling, has fewer mutations than the smaller ones—and these mutations have such a great effect and gain more and more usage . . . Concerning the mutations, we cannot praise the piano builders enough, who have worked tirelessly for years to add a large number of these to the instrument . . . But they are not used enough by the players, and so resemble a large book collection in which no one reads.[38]

He then praises Steibelt as the pianist who first accorded the mutations their proper place, and provides six pages of musical examples illustrating the use of the four pedals (harp,[39] damper, swell-box,[40] shift) in various combinations. His instructions for imitating little bells, Spanish music, a small drum, a glass harmonica, and other effects depend heavily on tremolos and repeated notes as well as the pedals; these too were staples of Steibelt's technique and his once-fashionable pieces. The opposing position was expressed perfectly in a review of this very treatise:

> This must be the worst chapter in the whole work. The author recommends the purchase of small square pianos—why? Because there are more stops and mutations on them! . . . We Germans would rather stick by our Stein instruments, on which one can do everything without stops.[41]

But even the Stein piano had a knee lever to raise the dampers, and, within a decade of this review, most German pianos had pedals for the dampers, moderator, *una corda*, and other effects. Conflicting attitudes towards the pedal can be seen in Czerny's statement that "Hummel's partisans accused Beethoven of mistreating the piano, of lacking all cleanness and

Example 4.24. Hummel, Musical examples from the original German edition of *Anweisung*, pp. 452–53.

Example 4.24.—*(concluded)*

clarity, of creating nothing but confused noise the way he used the pedal."[42] Unsurprisingly, the section on pedaling in Hummel's treatise begins by complaining about the widespread overuse of the pedal. He goes on to say: "though a truly great artist has no occasion for pedals to work upon his audience by expression and power, yet the use of the damper pedal has an agreeable effect in many passages . . . I shall insert here a few cases in which the damper pedal may be resorted to with the least breach of propriety."[43]

The tremolos, wide arpeggios, crossed-hand figures, and repeated chords in Hummel's examples (reproduced in Example 4.24)—techniques for prolonging a single harmony—each have their counterparts in Beethoven's writing, and it seems reasonable to infer that he, too, expected the pedal to be used in such passages. Especially noteworthy are the passing tones in measure 5 of the *Adagio* example; many pianists today might indeed find a certain "breach of propriety" in that bar. Note that the *Adagio* example also involves elaborate use of the soft pedal (*"Aufgehobene Dämpfung mit dem Pianozug,"* raised dampers with the soft pedal), notated with a small triangle.

Beethoven's Pedal Indications

The long pedal specified by Beethoven at the beginning of the last movement of the "Waldstein" sonata, with its low bass note, arpeggios, and crossed hands, resembles Hummel's examples. Contemporary pianists following Hummel's advice would certainly have pedaled here, but Beethoven's wish for a long pedal that blurs tonic and dominant harmonies required explicit notation (see Example 4.25). On the modern piano with its longer sustain, subtle partial pedal changes may be needed to produce the effect that Beethoven expected. But some blur is essential!

Example 4.26 is from the same movement. Any pianist, whether of our day or Beethoven's, would likely use the pedal for these arpeggios. But Beethoven has something special in mind: he wants a single pedal for the two *fortissimo* bars while most players would reflexively change at the barline—and, as I understand his directions, he wants the intervening *piano* bars played without pedal.[44]

Example 4.25. Beethoven, Sonata no. 21 in C major, "Waldstein, " op. 53, mvt. 3, mm. 1–9.

Example 4.26. Beethoven, Sonata no. 21 in C major, "Waldstein," op. 53, mvt. 3, mm. 441–48.

Example 4.27. Beethoven, Sonata no. 12 in A-flat major, op. 26, mvt. 3, mm. 31–32.

Example 4.27 is also unusual, and perhaps unclear because the modern "*" sign takes up less space than the words "*con sordini*". I hold the pedal until the *staccato* chords, without changing at the *f* in the middle of the bar.

The last movement of the "Moonlight" sonata (Example 4.28) proposes the reverse. The first part of the figure with the rapid notes is to be played dry, while the *sf* chords are to be pedaled, despite their staccato dots. Without Beethoven's explicit directions, the pedal could be maintained for each two-measure harmonic block. Or, the arpeggios could be played with pedal and the chords without, as in the previous example.

Example 4.28. Beethoven, Sonata no. 14 in C-sharp minor, "Moonlight," op. 27, no. 2, mvt. 3, mm. 1–4.

The three passages just discussed share a common characteristic: in each one Beethoven uses the pedal to reinforce a contrast that is already expressed by other elements of the music. In the "Waldstein" the pedaled music is loud and rising, while the unpedaled music is soft and descending. In the "Moonlight" the arpeggios are dry while the chords are pedaled, and in opus 26 the pedal is used with the tremolo in the low register, and the contrasting chords in the upper register are dry. For Beethoven the pedal is still a "register"—a special effect that calls attention to a passage or motive by imparting a distinctive color. He uses it strategically, and although some adaptation is required for the modern piano, this framework can lead to a more colorful and structured performance than a generalized, essentially uniform use of the pedal.

A Controversial Case: Czerny and the First Movement of the "Moonlight" Sonata

"*Si deve suonare tutto questo pezzo delicatissimamente e senza sordino*" ("One must play this entire piece with great delicacy and without dampers").[45] On some fortepianos it is just barely possible to play this famous opening movement all the way through without once changing the pedal.[46] It is a stunning effect, and its success depends as much on the "great delicacy" of the playing as on the undamped strings. But is this what Beethoven intended?

In his discussion of this movement—published in 1842, forty years after the sonata was composed—Czerny says *no*: "the prescribed pedal must be re-employed at each new note in the bass."[47] This is a plausible reading of Beethoven's instructions—one that could be paraphrased as "this entire piece uses the undamped register [with the necessary changes of pedal]." Was he reporting how Beethoven played the piece? Or might this advice reflect the impossibility of carrying out Beethoven's original plan on a piano of 1842? If Beethoven's "*senza sordino*" really meant no pedal changes at all for the entire movement, then perhaps this is the very piece that led "Hummel's partisans" to accuse Beethoven of "mistreating the piano, of lacking all cleanness and clarity, of creating nothing but confused noise the way he used the pedal."[48] Maybe it was too extreme even for his own student: Czerny was, after all, a conservative pedagogue. Personally, I try for the greatest amount of blur that I can stand on whatever piano I'm playing. On a modern piano, that means holding the pedal for the first two bars, then one pedal for each of the next two bars, and "messy" changes whenever possible (I also try to keep the pedal through the change from major to minor at m. 10).

I also disagree with Czerny's pedal suggestions for the first movement of the "Tempest" sonata. He says: "From the 21st bar, the pedal until the *piano*, and similarly at each *forte* of this passage, until the 41st bar . . . The

Example 4.29. Beethoven, Sonata no. 17 in D minor, "Tempest," op. 31, no. 2, mvt. 1, mm. 21–28 (showing both Czerny's and my pedal suggestions).

succeeding *Allegro* [of the development section] very impetuous, with the pedal at each *forte*."[49] I prefer the reverse, playing the *forte* arpeggio without pedal, and then pedaling the plaintive answer. Example 4.29 shows both Czerny's and my proposals.

My inspiration comes from measure 99, where the $\textit{\textbf{ff}}$ coincides with Beethoven's pedal release sign (Example 4.30).

Example 4.30. Beethoven, Sonata no. 17 in D minor, "Tempest," op. 31, no. 2, mvt. 1, mm. 95–101.

Of course there is no "right answer"; you may prefer Czerny's suggestion, or another solution entirely.

Transferring Beethoven's Long Pedals to the Modern Piano

Some of Beethoven's very long pedals create an especially blurred effect at the modern piano. These (Example 4.31), again from the "Tempest" sonata, are particularly striking:

Example 4.31. Beethoven, Sonata no. 17 in D minor, "Tempest," op. 31, no. 2, mvt. 1, mm. 143–61.

I believe that Beethoven knew what he was doing, and that the result—on pianos that he was familiar with—was just what he intended. Some adjustment is needed at the modern piano, but by just a bit of "cheating" with partial pedal changes, I can maintain the blur without creating ugly confusion. Banowetz devotes an entire chapter to this problem, in which he also considers more elaborate schemes involving the middle pedal.[50] For me, the least satisfactory of his proposals is to pedal exactly as indicated by Beethoven, but then deliberately *not* shape the line expressively, to avoid having notes stick out. This approach seems absolutely backwards to me. If instead we begin by discovering the deeply expressive effect that Beethoven's instructions produced on the instrument he knew—by playing or listening to a fortepiano—it's not difficult to produce a comparable effect on a modern piano.

Other long, "blurry" pedals that will respond to the same treatment can be found in the first movement of the sonata op. 57, measures 233–37; the second movement of op. 101, measures 30–34; and numerous passages in the Fourth Concerto. Depending on the piano, some adjustment may be useful in the last movement of the "Waldstein" as well.

Where Beethoven has not indicated any pedaling—which is to say, most of the time—we are left with more questions. But once we recognize Beethoven's taste for this kind of effect, and the ease with which it could be produced on his pianos, we can use it in many other passages. One student experienced this with the opening of opus 28. At the modern piano he had been changing the pedal with each measure, but at the fortepiano he preferred longer pedals—two measures or more between changes. He recognized that this pattern could not be transferred to the modern piano directly, but achieved a similar effect by actively compensating for the longer resonance (using half-changes, or depressing the pedal only partially). In his words: "the soundscape created on one keyboard [with a long pedal] can be deliberately evoked on the other."

Rhythmic vs. Syncopated (or Legato) Pedaling

Hummel's examples all describe rhythmic pedaling, where the pedal is depressed simultaneously with the bass note, while modern pianists

Example 4.32. Beethoven, Sonata no. 21 in C major, "Waldstein," op. 53, mvt. 3, mm. 251–58.

generally use syncopated pedaling instead, for the reasons discussed in Chapter 2 (see pp. 21–22).[51] Yet in passages like the one shown in Example 4.32, rhythmic pedaling suits the modern piano every bit as well as the fortepiano.

This time Beethoven notated it explicitly—presumably to make sure the bass note is sustained despite the jumping left hand—but it can also be used where no pedaling is notated, as in Example 4.33. Starting at measure 58, depress the pedal precisely with the long bass note, and release it (roughly) one beat before the next one. Notice that this creates an articulation before each of the octaves, highlighting the rhythmic aspect of the passage, while legato pedaling emphasizes continuity by smoothly connecting the bass line.

Crossed-hand passages require especially meticulous pedaling, as Czerny prescribes:[52]

> However, in order to produce this effect [of a third hand that sustains the bass notes while the left hand jumps], the player must press the pedal *precisely*

Example 4.33. Beethoven, Sonata no. 9 in E major, op. 14, no. 1, mvt. 3, mm. 58–66.

together with the octave [i.e., the bass, emphasis mine]; an instant too late and the pedal won't work and the octave will remain short and dry.

Since, additionally, this octave needs to sound through the entire measure, he must not release the pedal any sooner than with the last eighth note, in order to take the pedal again together with the next octave.[53]

Try Czerny's technique in this passage (Example 4.34). Be sure to follow his instructions to the letter.

Example 4.34. Beethoven, Sonata no. 3 in C major, op. 2, no. 3, mvt. 2, mm. 19–22.

In the previous phrase, similar but without the hand crossing, I pedal in just the same way to create articulation between the bass notes.

The Split Damper Pedal

On some English pianos it is possible to raise the bass and treble dampers independently. Until I had an opportunity to try an instrument with this capability, I imagined it would be useful primarily for sustaining a bass note while playing a melody containing passing tones or other non-harmonic notes, by raising only the bass dampers. (This would make it a precursor to the middle pedal of modern pianos.) Unexpectedly, I found the opposite effect much more interesting. Raising the treble dampers alone produced the pedal "atmosphere"—a gentle haze, or halo—without compromising the clarity of the harmony. Some surviving Viennese instruments also seem designed for this effect: the knee lever is split so

Example 4.35. Beethoven, Sonata no. 6 in F major, op. 10, no. 2, mvt. 1, mm. 19–29.

that the left side lifts all the dampers but the right side raises only the treble end of the rail. This lifts the treble dampers fully while the bass dampers function normally, with a half-pedaled effect for some notes in the middle. Beethoven was definitely aware of this system, because the autograph of opus 53 has a note explaining that wherever the *Ped.* indication appears, all of the dampers are to be raised, both bass and treble. Skowroneck[54] suggests that he may have had this technique in mind— raising the treble dampers only—for the performance of passages like the one shown in Example 4.35.

Following Skowroneck, I simulated this effect by inserting a wedge under the treble end of my Walter's damper rail.[55] It works very well; the melody soars while the left hand is gently blurred. At the modern piano I approximate this sound by holding the pedal down around a quarter of the way, and then partially clearing it for the harmony change.

Pedal: Conclusions

The pedal can be used to create a much broader range of effects than we usually employ in this repertoire. By avoiding (or reducing) pedal we may refine our articulation, while also producing contrast with surrounding passages that do use pedal. And by increasing the pedal to the point of producing effects that might seem "impressionistic," we can recover sounds that were evidently also part of the early nineteenth century's sound world. The clean, consistent pedaling that we prize today may well have struck musicians of the period as timid or prudish.

Case Study: Sonata in C Major, Op. 2, No. 3, First Movement

All of the topics discussed in the course of this chapter will now be brought to bear on this well-known movement.

The double thirds make the opening figure difficult to play cleanly, but I am primarily concerned with its grammar. The slur and the dots suggest that the two eighth notes form a distinct component and belong together; I try very hard not to make it sound like the 1935 Schnabel edition which slurs the first eighth to the previous sixteenth notes—"it is not at all the same," as Beethoven wrote to Holz.[56]

The difference is certainly clearer at the fortepiano, and the danger of creating an unmusical gap is greater at the modern piano, but if you are convinced by the distinction it isn't that difficult to produce. I use the following fingering:

5 4545 54 3 5
1 2121 12 1 1

Example 4.36. Beethoven, Sonata no. 3 in C major, op. 2, no. 3, mvt. 1, mm. 1–103.

Example 4.36.—*(continued)*

Example 4.36.—*(continued)*

Example 4.36.—*(concluded)*

Repeating 5–1 between the third and fourth beats ensures clear articulation of the eighth notes, as long as the foot is off the pedal. In the development section (mm. 117ff.) Beethoven further emphasizes this detail with *sf*. As an exercise, try Example 4.37 with the indicated fingering:

Example 4.37. Beethoven, Sonata no. 3 in C major, op. 2, no. 3, mvt. 1, mm. 117–18 (fingering added).

I play the opening, with its Mozartean mix of slurs and dots, as "classically" as possible, without any pedal. And to complement the only legato gesture in the passage—in the right hand at measure 7—I make sure to gently detach the left hand's quarter notes.

Measure 13 makes a clean break, with maximum contrast in dynamic, register, rhythm, and texture. The new material is also typical *pedal* music: tremolos and arpeggios prolonging a single harmony, just like Hummel's examples. Without pedal this passage can become empty bluster; I pedal it as heavily as possible—on some fortepianos, in the right acoustic, from measure 12 to measure 20 without changing. Even if changes or partial changes are necessary, I make sure that the pedal's resonance is a conspicuous feature of the passage. As in previous examples where the pedaling was notated by Beethoven himself, I want to point out and amplify the contrast inherent in the material. When the character changes at measure 21, I take the pedal off completely and play the sixteenths *non-legato* ("ordinary touch") both in the left-hand accompaniment, and, especially, in the scales at measure 25.

Slurs figure prominently in the G minor theme at measure 27. By using little or no pedal but plenty of overholding—in both hands—the detailed articulations in the melody can be projected clearly. (I assume that the one-measure slurs in the left hand are meant to continue *simile* at measure 31; the accents in that measure left the engraver no place to put the slur.) Reintroducing the pedal at the *dolce* of measure 47 provides a brand-new color, although this needn't preclude touches of pedal to reinforce the chords in measures 40 and 42.

Fingering is critical for projecting articulation. Example 4.38 compares the suggestions provided in two commonly used editions:

Example 4.38. Beethoven, Sonata no. 3 in C major, op. 2, no. 3, mvt. 1, mm. 29–30 (fingerings from Associated Board edition, left, and Henle, right).

The Associated Board edition's fingerings were supplied by David Ward, an experienced fortepianist, and his suggestion of 1–1 works perfectly on the fortepiano, with no pedal. On the modern piano the key travels so much deeper that the gap between the two notes played by the thumb may become too large (especially at the quick tempo that I prefer). If you like this fingering, you can use the pedal to minimize the gap, listening carefully to make sure the b♮^{1} is pronounced clearly. I prefer to play without pedal here, maintaining the contrast between the "normal" music (including this passage) and the "bluster" of the previous phrase, so I use this fingering:

1–2–4–2–5–4–2–1/2–5–4–1–3–2–1–2

This arrangement aligns the hand gestures with the slurs, and gives me precise control over the degree of articulation between the measures. I disagree with Conrad Hansen's fingering for the Henle edition which—in order to connect the measures that Beethoven has so clearly separated—proposes an awkward stretch between f♯^{2} and c^2 (3–2 at the end of m. 29).

Beethoven is consistent. The two slurs are repeated with every recurrence of this material: in the very next phrase at measure 35 and at the corresponding spots in the recapitulation, a total of four times. And their purpose seems clear: the slurs bring out the underlying descending line (more detail in the box, below). Furthermore, as we have seen in earlier examples, Beethoven does mark longer slurs when he wants them; there is a five-measure slur just ahead at measure 51.

More reasons for articulating between measures 29 and 30 (see Example 4.38)

By breaking the slur at the end of measure 29, Beethoven makes it clear that the b^1 at the beginning of measure 30 is not related to the c^2 which immediately precedes it, but rather to the same pitch, c^2, at the beginning of measure 29. Thus the arpeggiation of measure 29 is ornamental, not melodic, and the "real" line in this passage is the chromatic descent which begins with d^2 in measure 27, reaching a^1 in measure 32, at the rate of one pitch per bar. At this point there is a register shift and the descent continues, chromatically from a^2 to e^2, finally dropping diatonically through d^2 to c^2.

What about the dynamic shape inside each slur? The diminuendo principle that I insisted on in earlier examples doesn't satisfy me here because of the rising lines inside the slurs (measures 27 and 29). And a crescendo in measure 29 and diminuendo in the following bar—a seemingly natural shape for those two measures—create a "bulge" that obscures the longer line of which they are a part. I try to have it both ways, following the rising shape, then falling back again so that the end of the slur is weak, just as the theorists prescribe.[57] That enables what I'm really after—a clear beginning for the next slur.

At measure 47 I try not to pedal too cleanly, using the hazy sound, a slightly slower tempo, and generous *rubato* to give this theme its *dolce* character. Starting with the *forte* of measure 61, I use rhythmic pedaling, even on a modern piano, lifting the foot at the last quarter note of measures 62, 64, and 66, and then at every fourth eighth note in measures 67 and 68.

I play measures 69–72 without any pedal—dry and clangy—then, in measures 73–75, I oppose a dry octave in the left hand with a pedaled arpeggio in the right. On the fortepiano, the broken octaves from measure 85 work well with lots of pedal, changing at most each half bar; on the modern piano this effect requires subtle fluttering of the pedal. Further examples of the use of pedal as a special register to enhance contrast occur both in the development section and in the coda. The arpeggios in measures 97ff. and later in 218–32 may be just the sort of passages C. P. E. Bach had in mind when he recommended the undamped register for improvisation.

The second and third movements also provide opportunities of this kind; perhaps Beethoven was deliberately experimenting with a structural role for the pedal in this sonata. I avoid pedal from the beginning of the slow movement until the key-change at measure 11, then pedal heavily until the return of the opening material at measure 43 (this includes the crossed-hand passage discussed above). And I play the Scherzo entirely without pedal, to maximize the contrast with the Trio where I use as much pedal as possible.

&♭ &♭ &♭

Musical taste has changed a great deal since Beethoven's time, and we will never recapture the styles of performance that predate recorded sound. This is certainly no tragedy: we have our own styles now. But we pride ourselves on our sincere desire to understand other cultures, and we are indeed quite distant from Beethoven's Vienna. By appreciating the pianos that were part of his life we can get a little closer, opening our ears and minds to possibilities hidden in the most familiar works.

Chapter Five

Schubert

After exploring a variety of repertoire on all the instruments in my studio, visitors often find the combination of Schubert and the Graf the most compelling. In this short chapter, I will try to account for this reaction, while touching on several issues peculiar to the pianos of the 1820s.

A Multiplicity of Pedals

Most of Schubert's piano music was written when pianos had a range of at least six octaves, and just as many pedals—or even more. The instrument pictured below (Figure 5.1) has six: *shift* (*una corda*), which offers distinctly different sounds when depressed fully (the hammers hit only one string) or partially (for the sound of two strings); *bassoon*—this one controls a roll of parchment that, when lowered onto the bass strings, makes the piano buzz like a kazoo; the usual *damper* pedal; a *single moderator* and a *double moderator* (these bring one or two layers of felt cloth between the hammers and the strings); and the "*Turkish*" or "*Janissary*" pedal (a miniature percussion section, with a drumstick that strikes the soundboard and a set of bells). My own Graf copy has "only" four, lacking the bassoon and Turkish pedals. I never thought I'd miss those until I heard a performance of Schubert's *Divertissement à la Hongroise* that sounded like a full-fledged Hungarian folk ensemble.[1]

Moderators began to disappear by the 1830s, although a moderator-like "practice mute" is still offered on some modern upright pianos. Because the practice mute is made of felt, like the hammers themselves, it makes a quieter version of the regular sound. But on the older pianos with leather-covered hammers, the felt moderator produces a dramatically different sound: darker, veiled, even spooky. It can have a magical effect if not overused; András Schiff

Figure 5.1. Piano by Mathias Jakesch, ca. 1825. Collection of the Ira Brilliant Beethoven Center, San Jose, CA.

calls it the fortepiano's "secret weapon."[2] Videos on the website https://boydellandbrewer.com/piano-playing-revisited-hb.html show the moderator mechanism.

Four Hands and Four Feet

Four-handed piano playing was very fashionable in the 1820s. Schubert and others composed original music for piano four-hands; arrangements of symphonic and chamber music pieces were also popular. Perhaps these pianos were intended *primarily* for four-handed playing: their six-and-a-half-octave range provides more space for two players than earlier instruments with a smaller range did, and the puzzling arrangement of the pedals makes perfect sense if it was designed for four feet. Pianos with six or seven pedals generally have the damper control situated in the middle, with the *una corda* and the bassoon at the left, and the moderator(s) and the drum on the right. In four-handed (i.e., four-footed) playing, the damper pedal is in the ideal location for the right foot of the person playing the bottom part. A solo player, however, would have to operate the damper pedal with the left foot to use the moderator or the drum, and then switch back to the right in order to operate the *una corda* pedal or the bassoon. It can be done, but it's very clumsy. Modern-day owners of these pianos often cross the wires so that the damper pedal is on the extreme right, or simply disconnect some of the pedals entirely.

Schubert's Use of the Pedals

We can only speculate about how Schubert used the pedals, since the evidence is both scant and ambiguous. Here are some of the markings he used:

con sordini

"Sordino" (plural "sordini") means "mute" and we have already seen that Beethoven used the term to refer to the dampers. In Example 5.1 it most likely indicates the moderator, or perhaps, in conjunction with the *ppp* dynamic, the double moderator.

Example 5.1. Schubert, Sonata in A minor, op. 143/D. 784, mvt. 2, mm. 1–5.

mit Verschiebung

"Verschiebung" means "shifting" and refers to the pedal which shifts the keyboard, meaning the *una corda* pedal. This indication occurs in the song "Suleika," D. 740 (1821), in conjunction with a *pp* dynamic mark. The instruction is not without problems, however: the song eventually grows to a *ff* climax, and Schubert never cancels the "mit Verschiebung" instruction. Perhaps the *una corda* should be released when the crescendo begins, and taken again with the return of *pp* on the last page of the song.

pp mit erhobene Dämpfung

"*pp* with raised damping," meaning with the damper pedal. This can be found in the song "Sei mir gegrüsst," D. 741 (1822). The damper pedal was often referred to as the "forte pedal," but some writers remarked that it could also produce a noteworthy effect in quiet dynamics, as Schubert specifies in this song. As in the "Moonlight" sonata, there is no indication of when to lower the dampers. I presume that Schubert expected the pedal to be changed with the harmonies, i.e., every one or two measures.

durchaus mit dem Pianissimo (Example 5.2)

This intriguing marking ("throughout with the *pianissimo*") appears in the song "Morgenlied," D. 685 (1820).

Example 5.2. Schubert, "Morgenlied," D. 685, mm. 1–5.

"With 'the' pianissimo" suggests a device, not a playing technique; he would otherwise have written "durchaus *pianissimo*." It is most plausibly a direction to use some kind of soft pedal, and since he uses "Verschiebung" elsewhere to refer to the *una corda*, I assume that in this case he wants the moderator (single or double). And if Schubert associated the moderator with the *pianissimo* dynamic, perhaps he expected the moderator to be used in other places marked *pp*, as in Example 5.3.

To further complicate matters, some sources reserve the term "pianissimo pedal" for the *double* moderator, calling the (single) moderator the "piano"

Example 5.3. Schubert, Sonata in A minor, op. 143/D. 784, mvt. 1, mm. 244–49.

pedal.[3] Schubert never used "*mit dem Piano*" as an instruction, but he does occasionally write ***ppp***—perhaps he wanted the double moderator in those cases (although not every piano had one).

Schiff's characterization of the moderator as his "secret weapon" is not hyperbole. One of my students played the slow movement of Schubert's A minor sonata, op. 120 (see Example 5.4), on the Graf, and put it beautifully: "when I played the [*pianissimo*] opening with the moderator, the piece completely changed. The character of calmness and romantic serenity was suddenly so present. I was amazed that a simple pedal could completely change the whole atmosphere of a piece. This incredibly luminous and intimate atmosphere was nearly impossible to recreate on the modern piano."

Example 5.4. Schubert, Sonata in A major, op. 120/D. 664, mvt. 2, mm. 1–6.

It is indeed difficult to find a substitute for the moderator, but not totally impossible, as we shall see.

Elements of Performance

Tempo

The modern piano tempts many players to choose a very slow speed for Example 5.4. Artists such as Richter, Arrau, and Pletnev achieve a timeless, contemplative effect in this movement with tempi as slow as ca. ♩ = 36–40, but such interpretations are impossible on an instrument of Schubert's time. At the fortepiano, especially with the moderator which further reduces the instrument's resonance, ♩ = 60–63 produces a natural flow with a gentle lilt.

The student quoted above—who had been playing quite slowly on the modern piano—also favored a much faster tempo when playing at the fortepiano. Returning to the modern piano, she played faster than she had previously, but not as fast as at the fortepiano. Her "compromise" tempo (more like those of Kempff, Brendel, or Schiff, roughly ♩ = 52–55) helped to recreate the "calmness and romantic serenity" that she heard when playing with the moderator.

Example 5.5 is another *Andante*—this time *alla breve*—that is often played quite slowly on the modern piano, but which moves easily and comfortably at a quicker pace on the historical instrument. A student who had been trying to play this at ♩ = 62 on the modern piano found 68–70 very comfortable on the Graf. Turning back to the modern piano again prompted a compromise in the tempo, as well as some very careful pedaling to maintain clarity in the melody.

Example 5.5. Schubert, Drei Klavierstücke, D. 946, no. 1, mm. 118–21.

Texture

Schubert's use of the top octave

A big surprise for modern pianists when they first encounter the Graf is the thin, silvery sound of the top octave. It seems delicate and fragile, without much punch or sustaining power. Schubert's use of this register takes this weakness into account, sometimes reinforcing the top line with octave doubling, as in Example 5.6 from the "Trout" quintet, or using the distinctive color to create a charming "music box" effect, as in Example 5.7, from his Sonata in G major, D.894.

Example 5.6. Schubert, Piano Quintet in A major, "Trout," D. 667, mvt. 1, mm. 114–15.

Example 5.7. Schubert, Sonata in G major, D. 894, mvt. 1, mm. 39–42.

Similar effects are especially common in the four-hand works (see Example 5.8), which typically make more use of the top and bottom of the piano than a two-handed piece.

Example 5.8. Schubert, Allegro in A minor, "Lebensstürme," op. 144/D. 947, mm. 138–42.

It's not difficult to produce the requisite charm on a modern piano (a relaxed hand, a comfortable tempo, and a determined effort *not* to project those high notes), but hearing these effects on historical instruments suggests another reason why Schubert wrote in this way. They give the impression that these passages are *far away*—in the sense of being both distant from the listener, and distant from the musical activity in the lower parts of the piano. To recreate this spatial dimension on a modern instrument I combine a quiet dynamic with extremely clear articulation.

Melody and Accompaniment

Schubert's piano pieces, no less than his *Lieder*, are as notable for the richness and variety of the accompaniment figures as for the originality of the melodies and harmonies. In the piano music, where the player is responsible for both melody and accompaniment, balancing these elements can be a challenge—particularly on a modern piano. It's easier on the Graf, because the distinct timbre of each register gives the individual parts their own character. Even with the pedal down, the separate strands of the music retain their individuality, like the members of a woodwind quintet. The melodies are less lush and sustained than at a modern piano, but every register can be heard clearly. This ideal was described by Streicher in his pamphlet of 1801,[4] and repeated verbatim by Dieudonné and Schiedmayer in 1824:[5] "the tones of a fortepiano, sounding alone or together, should as much as possible resemble the best wind instruments, if they are to arouse pleasure or move one's feelings."

The Graf's thin, clear, bass and its reedy-sounding tenor register are especially helpful in achieving a satisfying balance with the upper part. These qualities make a big difference in two kinds of textures. The first is rhythmically active accompaniments, whether in the left hand of a piano piece (as in Example 5.9), or in both hands of a song accompaniment (as in Example 5.10):

Example 5.9. Schubert, Drei Klavierstücke, D. 946, no. 1, mm. 1–6.

Example 5.10. Schubert, "Halt!" from *Die schöne Müllerin*, D. 795, no. 2, mm. 21–26.

On the Graf the individual notes can be played clearly, which adds rhythmic energy. On a modern piano it's tempting to reduce these parts to a smooth hum; extra effort is required to preserve the vitality of the accompaniment while keeping it from overwhelming the melody.

The second kind of texture, especially problematic on the modern piano, is when there are passing tones over pedaled bass notes, often combined with repeated chords (as in Example 5.11):

Example 5.11. Schubert, Impromptu in B-flat major, op. 142/D. 935, no. 3, mm. 55–56.

At the Graf there is no problem. With just one pedal change for each bass note, everything remains clear: the tension created by the non-harmonic tones—e♮ and g♭ in the left hand in the first bar shown—enhances the restless character of the variation without creating confusion. At the Steinway, this effect is elusive, and requires subtle pedaling (quick and/or partial changes) as well as careful control over the voicing of the chords. Hearing how such passages sound at the Graf can lead the way—but making that sound yourself on such an instrument is even better! Once you have a clear idea of the result, your ear will guide your hands and foot at a modern piano. And I'm comfortable sustaining the bass with the pedal, despite the staccato dots, since for Schubert—as we can see from Example 5.12—pedal is not inconsistent with the notion of a staccato touch. (The same is true for Beethoven: see the beginning of the last movement of the "Waldstein" sonata.) With the longer sustain of the modern piano, additional pedal changes are needed—but the bass notes should still resonate like a plucked string.

Example 5.12. Schubert, Trio in E-flat major, op. 100/D. 929, mvt. 2, mm. 56–58.

Although this example establishes that one *may* pedal a staccato bass note, I would not suggest that one *must* pedal every such texture. In the mournful slow movement of the A major sonata (Example 5.13), I prefer to highlight the sparseness of the texture by interpreting the dot literally and playing the bass short, without pedal. The right hand sings alone, while the left hand emphasizes the wide gap between the bass and tenor voices. If I pedal at all, it's only to smooth the octave (depressing the pedal on the second beat, releasing on the third). Go ahead and experiment—one cannot make a rule.

Example 5.13. Schubert, Sonata in A major, D. 959, mvt. 2, mm. 1–8.

Case Study, Impromptu, Op. 90, No. 1

I had struggled with this piece for a long time at the modern piano, and was truly amazed at how many of the difficulties simply disappeared at the fortepiano (see Examples 5.14, 5.15, and 5.16).

- The *ff* of the opening bar seemed to go on forever on the modern piano, after which it was hard to get the piece going. The Graf's relatively quick decay makes for a much more natural progression. I could approximate this effect at the modern piano by unobtrusively releasing the middle voices, while feathering the pedal. (It also helps not to play the lowest G too loud.)

- I always found the staccato chords in measures 5–8 too dry (if unpedaled), or too messy (with the pedal), and never quite the right length. The Graf's reedy tone color and slight "after-ring" gave this passage the natural expression I had been looking for. At the modern piano a very shallow press of the pedal (one-eighth of the way) for each chord helps create the same effect.

Example 5.14. Schubert, Impromptu in C minor, Op. 90/D. 899, no. 1, mm. 1–11.

- I had trouble with the pedaling in the passage from measure 42. At the Graf, pedaling with each harmony change works perfectly. The unaccented dissonances in the left hand don't get in the way, and the tune is always clear. I came closest to approximating this effect at the modern piano by playing the left hand slightly detached, and again using very shallow pedals.

Example 5.15. Schubert, Impromptu in C minor, Op. 90/D. 899, no. 1, mm. 41–46.

• The passage at measure 74 was an absolute nightmare: the repeated chords were much too thick, especially since I tried to keep the bass notes sounding through most of each measure. Again, the Graf showed me that Schubert did not intend it to be this difficult; one pedal for each measure produced just the effect I wanted. On the modern piano, I make sure that the left-hand chords are never depressed very deeply, while rapidly vibrating the pedal.

Example 5.16. Schubert, Impromptu in C minor, Op. 90/D. 899, no. 1, mm. 74–78.

- Finally, for the ***ppp*** at the very end, I was totally smitten by the effect of the moderator on the Graf: the music just fades into the distance. Surprisingly, I found that I could evoke a similar image on the modern piano by pulling the tempo back slightly. It seemed an unlikely equivalence—mimicking the sound of the moderator pedal by playing at a different speed—but not that dissimilar to the experience of the student playing opus 120, discussed above (p. 121). Once I "got" the effect of the moderator in this passage, finding another route to the same destination came easily.

❧   ❧   ❧

In his essay alluded to earlier in this chapter, András Schiff describes the evolution of his attitude towards historical instruments. His initial skepticism and resistance, reinforced by an unsatisfying experience with Beethoven's Broadwood (prior to its restoration), was followed by a revelatory experience with Mozart's Walter, and led eventually to his acquisition of an 1820 Viennese instrument by Brodmann which he calls "ideally suited to Schubert's keyboard works." He concludes the essay by asking:

> Does this mean that I'll never again play Schubert on a modern piano in a large concert hall? Quite to the contrary. I'll continue doing so on Bösendorfers, Bechsteins, Steinways, but the sweet tone of the Viennese fortepiano and its sound in a small hall will always remain in the back of my mind.

I carry that sound in the back of my mind too, and so can you.

Chapter Six

Chopin

On the piano, playing Chopin in a tasteful way requires one to walk a tightrope, with tasteless over-romanticism on one side, and square and sterile academia on the other. On the Pleyel, this tightrope expanded a bit, and there was some ease and comfort in interpretation.

—a student in my seminar at the Université de Montréal

Chopin on the Pleyel

The Pleyel brings us closer to Chopin. His affinity for these pianos is well-documented;[1] he used them for his Paris performances whenever possible and also in his teaching. They can help us interpret his highly prescriptive notation, now available in new, more accurate critical editions (such as Jan Ekier's for the Polish National Edition, and John Rink *et al.* for Peters). Accounts of his playing and teaching—conveniently organized and indexed by Eigeldinger—provide further insight into Chopin's style, as do recordings by pianists descended from the Chopin circle such as Raoul Koczalski, Raoul Pugno, and Moriz Rosenthal.

The new editions include alternate readings for many passages.[2] These variants complicate the editor's job but are a treasure trove for interpreters: besides giving us choices of what to play, they remind us that this music was born of improvisation. Yet despite their improvisatory origins, Chopin's scores are astonishingly specific, with meticulous instructions for dynamics, articulation, and pedaling. These contradictory traits of freedom and control are beautifully reflected in this description of Chopin's compositional process by his companion George Sand:

> His creativity was spontaneous, miraculous; he found it without seeking it, without expecting it. It arrived at his piano suddenly, completely, sublimely, or it sang in his head during a walk, and he would hasten to hear it again by

recreating it on his instrument. But then would begin the most heartbreaking labor I have ever witnessed . . . He would shut himself up in his room for days at a time, weeping, pacing, breaking his pens, repeating or changing a single measure a hundred times, writing it and erasing it with equal frequency, and beginning again the next day with desperate perseverance.[3]

The relevance of old instruments to our understanding of Chopin is beginning to be recognized. The Fryderyk Chopin Institute in Warsaw, in collaboration with Polish Television and Polish Radio, sponsored the first International Chopin Competition on Period Instruments in 2018; the competition is to take place every five years. According to the institute's press release, "approximating the original color and mechanics of the instruments the composer had at his disposal permits us to grasp the unique, specific character of Chopin's music, with its one-of-a-kind articulation and harmonic language, in large measure lost in interpretations on contemporary instruments."[4]

Elements of Performance

Scale

Unlike the earlier pianos whose smaller keys, shallow key dip, and light touch put my seminar students on their guard right away, the Pleyel seemed—at first—relatively familiar. But, in treating it like a modern piano, they quickly discovered its lack of power, or, put in a more positive light, its *fragility*, especially in the upper register. These qualities align with descriptions of Chopin's playing, particularly his sparing use of force and his mastery of nuance in the lower dynamic levels.[5] In this respect Chopin's style is the precise opposite of Liszt's. Unsurprisingly, Liszt preferred the Erard, which has much more in common with our modern pianos. The piano's development has promoted a tradition of "Liszt-ifying" Chopin that goes all the way back to Liszt himself, a situation captured perfectly in an anecdote which is probably untrue: Liszt thunders away at a piece by Chopin, who, upon hearing him, asks, "Whose piece is that?"

Two students had contrasting first impressions of the Pleyel; I appreciate the direct honesty of both.

It isn't possible to play as powerfully as on a modern piano. The sound becomes forced as soon as one presses at all on the keys. I can't imagine how one could play some of the études or one of Chopin's sonatas without splitting the piano in two.

> The best thing I loved right away about the Pleyel was that I did not have to worry about the piano sounding "too loud." I often worry that I play too loud on modern pianos, and I always want to hold back on a Yamaha because I am afraid it will sound harsh and out of control.

Because the Pleyel lacks the brute power to support long crescendos, it forces players to pay attention to micro-dynamics and other small-scale details. Here is a student who recognized that from the beginning: "[The Pleyel] is much quieter and more refined than what we're accustomed to from the modern piano. Therefore we have to adjust our perceptions and accept a lesser degree of contrast in the level of sound, varying the colors and musical intensity instead."

Chopin's own performances, most of which took place in Parisian salons, did not feature displays of pianistic power. The setting was intimate, listeners were near the piano, and there was no need to project to the "back of the balcony." We know that Chopin's health was compromised, so physical weakness might explain his preference for quiet subtleties and the avoidance of forceful effects. Still, it is equally plausible that those qualities would have characterized his music had he enjoyed perfect health. According to Chopin, "Concerts are never real music; you have to give up the idea of hearing in them the most beautiful things of art."[6]

Another of my students was inspired by the Pleyel almost immediately:

> I approached the Pleyel for the first time with no conscious preconceptions, and created my first sound in the same way that I would have on a modern instrument. This greeting was obviously in the wrong language and fell quite flat for the Pleyel, who responded in kind with what can only be described as a thud. My first attempt rejected, I considered a more sympathetic approach, gently trying to coax a pleasant sound from this delicate character. As I played, the Pleyel began to take me with it; I experienced an unavoidable urge to find more and more colors and to experiment more broadly with time and textures . . .

In the twentieth century, Chopin's music moved from the salon to the large concert hall, and from the Pleyel to the modern piano; both of these changes encouraged players to abandon subtlety in favor of large-scale dramatic effects. Paradoxically, since twenty-first-century listeners are more likely to encounter Chopin through headphones than in a public concert, we may be better equipped today to recapture the sensitivity and intimacy with which Chopin originally seduced his public.

Texture

As we have seen in other contexts, the modern piano excels at projecting a single voice surrounded by a harmonious, but discreet, accompaniment. In the typical texture of a Chopin nocturne—a sustained melody on top, a slow-moving bass on the bottom, and chordal or arpeggiated elements in the middle—this means voicing the melody strongly, connecting the bass notes with the pedal, and making the "filler" unobtrusively hazy in the background. The Pleyel, like virtually all pre-Steinway pianos, is less conducive to this style of playing. Its relatively weak upper register and generally quicker decay frustrate players who approach it with this sound ideal in mind. But Chopin's textures are perfectly calculated to counteract this apparent weakness. Since the individual registers of the Pleyel have distinctive timbres just like earlier pianos, it's easier to bring out the counterpoint; an artfully played accompaniment, given "equal billing" with the melody, becomes a powerful expressive tool.

One student used the expression "luminous clarity" to describe a performance on the Pleyel of the extraordinary passage shown in Example 6.1. The upper voices, each in its own register, have individual "sonic personalities," while the chromatic bass remains perfectly distinct.

Example 6.1. Chopin, Sonata no. 3 in B minor, op. 58, mvt. 1, mm. 23–26.

Chopin frequently uses a chorale texture in four or sometimes more voices (Ballade no. 2, Preludes no. 17 and 20, etc.). Because of the Pleyel's transparency, the individual notes can be voiced more equally than on a modern piano, making the chords fuller and denser without sacrificing clarity. The difference is especially pronounced when the chords come in the lower registers (e.g., Prelude no. 9). At the modern piano, with its crossed stringing and heavy wire in the bass, this kind of writing can easily become muddy, just as it does in the works of earlier composers (i.e., the closing measures of Mozart's K. 533, the beginning of Beethoven's "Waldstein" Sonata). The same principle applies to other thick textures, such as the F-sharp minor Prelude (Example 6.2):

Example 6.2. Chopin, Prelude in F-sharp minor, op. 28, no. 8, mm. 1–2.

Chopin's writing is very different from that of the classical composers but poses a similar challenge: projecting a well-focused melody without sacrificing the richness and complexity of the rest of the texture.

Tempo Choice

Chopin gave metronome marks for many of his pieces, yet today's performers often choose tempi vastly different from those he indicated. Metronome indications are problematic in the works of other composers, too. Brahms, for example, supplied and then withdrew metronome markings for the *German Requiem*. There are at least three explanations for these inconsistencies in tempo that do not depend on instruments:

1. Composers may try to determine the tempo while performing the music in their heads, rather than in "real life"; everything can happen faster in the mind, without the physical resistance of the real world.

2. Tempo choice depends on external factors, such as the acoustics of the room in which the music is played.

3. Speed depends on the temperament of the player; there can be no "one-size-fits-all" tempo.

Nevertheless, as we have seen in earlier chapters, the instrument also plays a role—above all in slow music. The sustaining power of the modern piano can inspire players to adopt tempi that would be impossibly slow on the Pleyel, but not without a cost: the melody may sound beautiful, but the accompaniment figures become sluggish, the harmonic progressions lose their force, and the rhythm becomes less flexible.

The D-flat major Nocturne (op. 27, no. 2) is often heard at a slower tempo than a historical piano would permit. Chopin's marking is ♩. = 50, i.e., ♪ = 150. This seems very quick for the beginning, although quite appropriate for the more active passages that come later. However, the piece is generally played at about ♪ = 80, almost twice as slowly as indicated! Beautiful performances have been recorded at even slower tempi: I greatly admire Ivan Moravec, who plays at around ♪ = 60, but I doubt that even he would choose that speed on a piano of Chopin's period.

The E-flat minor étude, op. 10, no. 6, is another example. The tempo marking is *Andante*, ♩. = 69, which is astonishingly fast, perhaps a mistake. The usual speed of ca. 30 or slower makes the melody almost impossible to follow on a piano with a quicker decay; I am most comfortable at about ♩. = 50. Of course this tempo won't work if played too rigidly, but Chopin's indication "*con molto espressione*" suggests a generous use of *rubato*.

Rubato and Tempo Flexibility

Chopin's handling of rhythm made a strong impression on his listeners, but their descriptions can seem contradictory. Some stressed the steadiness of his beat, others its flexibility. Here are two statements, both attributed to his student (and subsequently his teaching assistant) Karl Mikuli:

> In keeping time Chopin was inexorable, and some readers will be surprised to learn that the metronome never left his piano. Even in his much maligned tempo rubato, the hand responsible for the accompaniment would keep strict time, while the other hand, singing the melody, would free the essence of the musical thought from all rhythmic fetters, either by lingering hesitantly or by eagerly anticipating the movement with a certain impatient vehemence akin to passionate speech.[7]

Chopin was far from being a partisan to metric rigour and frequently used rubato in his playing, accelerating or slowing down this or that theme. But Chopin's rubato possessed an unshakeable emotional logic. It always justified itself by a strengthening or weakening of the melodic line, by harmonic details, by the figurative structure. It was fluid, natural; it never degenerated into exaggeration or affectation.[8]

These two contrasting reports correspond to what Richard Hudson calls the *earlier* and *later* types of rubato.[9] Each was current during Chopin's lifetime, and, as we can see from the accounts of Mikuli and others, he was a master of both. The later one, which involves speeding up and slowing down the overall tempo, is still widely practiced today. The earlier one, featuring a flexible melody over a steady accompaniment, can still be heard in popular music styles (where the rhythm section keeps steady time while a singer or instrumental soloist can push ahead or pull back) but is virtually extinct from current classical performance. It is described in the treatises of Quantz[10] and C. P. E. Bach,[11] and was also practiced by Mozart: "Everyone is amazed that I can always keep strict time. What these people cannot grasp is that in tempo rubato, in an Adagio, the left hand should go on playing in strict time."[12]

What happened to this style? First of all, it isn't easy to do. Camille Saint-Saëns described it, along with the pitfalls of attempting it, in an article published in 1911 [translation mine].

> Ah! Tempo rubato, what errors are committed in its name! Because it can be real or it can be fake, just as with jewels. In the real one, the accompaniment remains undisturbed while the melody floats capriciously, ahead or behind, sooner or later recovering its support. This type of execution is very difficult, demanding complete independence of the hands; and when you can't manage it, you give yourself and others the illusion that you are by dislocating the accompaniment, playing it at the wrong time; or, even worse—the last resort—simply playing the hands one after the other. It would be a hundred times better to play everything in time and together, but this wouldn't be "artistic."[13]

But perhaps more importantly, the modern, melody-centered approach has undermined the potency of that old-style rubato, which depends on the clarity and independence of the accompaniment. Chopin's pupil Wilhelm von Lenz described how that independence was to be acquired:

> [The left-hand part to the Nocturne in E-flat major, op. 9, no. 2] to be practiced first by itself, divided between the two hands . . . Once the bass part is

mastered—with two hands . . . *in strict time*, then the left hand can be entrusted with the accompaniment *played that way* and the tenor invited to sing his part in the upper voice [emphases mine].[14]

Saint-Saëns's "last resort," where a routine dislocation of the hands is just a tic, not the result of independent rhythms, can be heard on many early twentieth-century recordings; that style is no longer tolerated. Instead, we usually get something equally impoverished: an accompaniment that is perfectly synchronized but absolutely subservient.

I believe that the "left hand in strict time" as described by Mozart and echoed by Saint-Saëns is actually shorthand for something more interesting: an *illusion* of strictness while subtly adapting to the melody's needs. Chopin's recipe as described by Lenz—perfecting a stable, independent accompaniment before adding the melody—is the surest route to that goal, at any piano.

Pedaling

"Chopin made the most detailed pedal indications of any composer; too bad they're all wrong." This remark was attributed to the late, great pianist Egon Petri, and although I haven't been able to authenticate the quote, I suspect many thoughtful pianists would agree with the sentiment. Most composers, like Beethoven, only give pedal instructions when they have something special in mind. Many of Chopin's compositions, on the other hand, have a continuous set of pedal indications, often measure after measure with the same style of pedaling—perhaps because he had his students in mind, and wanted to show them exactly what to do.

Saint-Saëns took a hard line:

> The pedal is very important in Chopin. Many people, seeing that it is very frequently indicated by the composer, think it should be used continually; this is a big mistake: Chopin indicated it often because he wanted it used where he indicated it, and nowhere else. [15]

Yet many of the markings seem puzzling, if not infuriating, and—as the Petri quote suggests—most players ignore them. The problem is compounded because we all recognize (Petri too, presumably) that the pedal is an important ingredient in Chopin's style, so we want to do it right. I hope to persuade you that the historical approach holds the key to this riddle, and that it can open our eyes and ears to qualities of Chopin's music that are usually hidden.

Many students encountering the Pleyel for the first time began with observations about the pedal. Some noticed that it is possible to play with less pedal; others pointed out the reverse. Both responses make sense. Less pedal works because the Pleyel's slightly "leaky" dampers provide a subtle halo of resonance all the time; more pedal (i.e., longer stretches without changing the pedal) also works because the dissonances, like all the other notes, decay more quickly.

These differences are sufficient to account for the strangeness of many of Chopin's markings, and to disclose some of their secrets: clues hidden in plain sight.[16] Pianists have certainly looked at them before, but because they produce such unsatisfactory results on a modern piano, even the best-intentioned players eventually give up. Once we recognize that the problem originates with our pianos, not with Chopin's instructions, we can see the scores with fresh eyes. Even though the indications cannot be followed exactly at the modern piano, it's worth studying them meticulously because they reveal Chopin's thinking.[17] In the following section I will categorize the pedalings by their function, show how Chopin's directions work on the Pleyel, and suggest strategies for realizing his intentions on a modern piano.

Pedal for Contrast

Example 6.3, the opening of the second sonata, shows three kinds of pedal indications in quick succession, making it a useful starting point for this discussion:

1. The first four bars have no instructions. I do not agree with Saint-Saëns's suggestion that the pedal may be used only where Chopin has indicated it and "nowhere else," so we're on our own here; Chopin has left us to our instincts and our taste. (I don't think it's possible to go far wrong.)

2. At *Doppio movimento* Chopin asks for three long pedals, three or four bars each. Although many pianists may obey the first one, the temptation to "clean up" the blur that begins at the *Agitato* is very strong—even at the Pleyel, which produces a considerably clearer effect here than a modern piano. But that blur contributes to the agitation of the passage, and it isn't difficult to produce something comparably "dirty" at the modern piano by using half-changes or partial-pedaling.

Example 6.3. Chopin, Sonata no. 2 in B-flat minor, op. 35, mvt. 1, mm. 1–21.

3. Starting at measure 16 we find a series of short pedals—rhythmic pedaling, with gaps—that produce a different, breathless kind of agitation. The sound is cleaner, but both the dissonance level and the dynamic level have risen. The last measure shown, the climax of the phrase, has a full-measure pedal, and is the loudest and "dirtiest."

If we replace Chopin's carefully calculated instructions with ordinary, regular pedal changes we iron out his deliberate effects, leaving only a smooth surface.

The contrast between pedaled and unpedaled sound shown in Example 6.4 underpins the basic structure of the Mazurka, op. 63, no. 3. While Chopin prescribes pedal for every bar of the opening section and its return, the middle section has virtually none. Perhaps we're on our own here too, and meant to pedal freely. Paderewski evidently thought so; his edition "corrects" Chopin by supplying the "missing" markings. But the evidence favors reading the directions literally: for the three spots where the bass cannot be sustained by the fingers Chopin provides the necessary short pedal indications, and—remarkably—the other Mazurkas of op. 63 use pedal in just the same way.[18] (And *sotto voce* at m. 33 could be an invitation to switch from the right pedal to the left pedal.)

The Impromptu, op. 29, provides an elegant summary of the different ways Chopin uses pedal to create contrast and underline structure. It's an especially instructional example because the autograph reveals changes to the pedaling made at a late stage of the compositional process. In the following examples (6.5, 6.6, and 6.7) Chopin's crossed-out markings are indicated with X.

We begin with some strange-looking pedal markings in the middle section, shown in Example 6.5. Note the gaps. Between measures 35 and 46, pedal is specified for only part of every bar. The inconsistency is jarring, but it isn't difficult to discern a pattern. Starting with measure 36, Chopin alternates dominant and tonic harmonies; each of the *dominant* harmonies is pedaled, the resolving, *tonic* harmonies are always unpedaled. The contrasting colors of "pedal-on" and "pedal-off" serve to reinforce the contrasting harmonic functions, recalling C. P. E. Bach's view of the pedal as a special register. The crossed-out markings in measure 42 prove that the gaps are not oversights but rather explicit instructions *not* to pedal; perhaps Chopin only recognized the logic of the arrangement later, and adjusted the pedaling to make the passage more consistent.

Example 6.4. Chopin, Mazurka in C-sharp minor, op. 63, no. 3, mm. 25–48.

At the *ritenuto* in measure 46 the pattern changes. The diminished harmony alters the atmosphere completely, and the pedaling changes too. After three fully pedaled bars, "pedal-off" (from the second beat of m. 49 until the downbeat of m. 51) marks the transition to the new section. The seemingly haphazard indications conceal a careful design that deploys pedal strategically for two distinct purposes: underlining the harmony, and articulating the structure.

At the modern piano the unpedaled bits are almost certainly too dry, but they don't sound dry at all on most nineteenth-century pianos, including my ca. 1870 Bösendorfer. (Strategies for realizing Chopin's intentions on today's

Example 6.5. Chopin, Impromptu in A-flat major, op. 29, mm. 35–52 (large Xs indicate pedal marks crossed out in the autograph).

Example 6.6. Chopin, Impromptu in A-flat major, op. 29, mm. 1–30.

Example 6.6.—*(concluded)*

instruments will be discussed below, in the section entitled Returning to the Modern Piano.)

Turning now to the beginning of the Impromptu (Example 6.6), we find a third purpose for the pedal-on/pedal-off contrast: reinforcing the meter. In the first two bars, the pedal is on for the strong beats, and off for the weak beats. The next two bars show the same contrast, but this time at the whole-measure level: measure 3—the strong bar—has pedal throughout, while the next has none. Note the relocated pedal-release in measure 3; once again Chopin has made a change that strengthens the symmetry of his design. The next four bars repeat the first ones, but with no pedal indications. Chopin might have been counting on us to repeat the pedaling as well, but a literal reading would extend the pedal-on/pedal off contrast to the next level. This works beautifully on the Pleyel; on the Steinway a light sheen of shallow pedal can suggest the same effect.

In the section that follows, measures 9–20, Chopin uses double stems to prescribe finger-pedaling. The actual pedal is indicated only when the fingers cannot sustain the bass, just like the *sotto voce* section in Example 6.4. The return of "pedal-on" at the crescendo in measure 21 is another example of "pedal to articulate structure." This is the climactic passage of the piece and has the most heavily pedaled music (ten consecutive bars), including one unusually long pedal filled with non-harmonic tones at measures 25–26 (again, the result of an emendation visible in the autograph). At measures 27–30, the repeating pattern provides another example of "pedal used to underline the harmony."

But I am most struck by a pedal effect in the coda, underlined by one more revision shown in the autograph (see Example 6.7). A four-bar phrase is repeated (mm. 113–19), but by crossing out a single pedal marking Chopin gives the swirling triplets two contrasting expressions: active and articulate, then dying away (*pp*) in a haze of pedal.

And yet the publication history of the piece suggests that he had mixed feelings about this effect: the English edition has long pedals both times, the French edition has just the short pedals on the chords, while only the German edition presents the contrast that we see here. Perhaps he was taking each market into account, catering especially to the English taste for long-held pedals already recognized and imitated by Haydn in 1796. Perhaps he continued to change his mind, revising the pedaling as each copy was sent out for publication. Or the differences may reflect choices—or simply oversights—by the editor or engraver at each publishing house.

Personally, I find the contrasting pedalings (mm. 113–14 vs. 117–18) an inspired touch. The dynamics already create an echo effect; the pedal adds resonance exactly as a real echo does. And it makes a "literal" reading of measures 1–8 even more attractive, by bracketing the piece with a similar device at both ends. As if to drive home the point, the final bars juxtapose dry and wet one last time: complementary modes to be balanced just like *forte* and *piano*, dissonance and consonance.

No Marking = No Pedal?

At this point it may appear that I'm endorsing Saint-Saëns's position after all; so far, the only exception has been the introductory bars of the Sonata

Example 6.7. Chopin, Impromptu in A-flat major, op. 29, mm. 111–27 (large Xs indicate pedal marks crossed out in the autograph).

op. 35. But the situation is not that simple. The first section of the Second Ballade provides a compelling counterexample. The opening forty-six measures have only two pedal markings. In this piece Chopin, like Beethoven, seems to have marked only those spots where he wants a very particular effect (see Example 6.8). The initial long pedal reinforces the floating quality of the opening, preventing the articulation of a clear downbeat until the third bar; at measure 45 the pedaling ensures that the bass is sustained as long as possible. The likelihood that we are supposed to convey continuous legato (indicated with extra-long slurs) for the intervening forty-two measures with no pedal at all seems remote.

Example 6.8. Chopin, Ballade no. 2 in F major, op. 38, mm. 1–9, 43–45.

There are many similar examples: the Etude in E major, op. 10, no. 3, has exactly three pedal markings in the entire piece; op. 10, no. 4, in C-sharp minor, has only one, at the very end. Perhaps Chopin or his publishers had a pedagogical motivation for supplying very complete pedaling in some pieces, while in others we are "on our own" at least some of the time. Or maybe the reason was practical: some of the passages without indications might require pedal techniques that Chopin used but could not easily notate—syncopated pedaling, perhaps, but also subtle effects such as very quick pedals, partial pedals, or flutter pedaling.

We are still left wondering what Chopin might have expected contemporary players, including his students, to do "on their own," but the printed indications suggest that their practices were quite different from ours. Our approach—dampers raised as much as possible, with unnoticeable pedal changes keeping the bass line connected and the harmonies clean—may have developed in response to changes in instrument design, but it also fits with a general preference in the twentieth century for smooth, regular shapes, like the Bauhaus style discussed in Chapter 1.

Pedal for Articulation

Pedal and its absence can convey breathing or articulation between individual gestures, as in Example 6.9. Chopin's pedaling makes the opening figure rhythmic and rhetorical, with an articulation between the first and second beats. The placement of the pedal release sign at the end of each measure suggests a breath between the bars, as well.

Unusual pedaling also adds complexity to the opening bars of the Fourth Ballade (Example 6.10). The piece begins with repeated octaves, pedaled, crescendo. Chopin asks for the pedal to be released part-way through this gesture,[19] allowing the tenor voice to fade away (a diminuendo fork is indicated for the left hand), before the return of the pedal with the bass's entrance marks the "real" beginning of the piece. How much more interesting this is than a "normal" pedaling, with its consistent, clean texture! (On a modern piano, however, some very light pedal might be required to keep the first half of m. 2 from sounding too dry.)

Example 6.11 shows another instance of pedaling for articulation. Compare measures 70–72 with 78–80. The subtle difference in pedaling supports the changes in slurring, as well as the placement of the accents on the bb²s. As I interpret it, the motive is more delicate the first time. The pedal "breath" at the end of measure 70 encourages me to play the next measure gently (I take both notes at the end of the measure with my right hand,

Example 6.9. Chopin, Polonaise-fantaisie in A-flat major, op. 61, mm. 1–2.

Example 6.10. Chopin, Ballade no. 4 in F minor, op. 52, mm. 1–3.

Example 6.11. Chopin, Ballade no. 1 in G minor, op. 23, mm. 66–80.

to avoid a big gap in the bass). The second time, the new slur in measure 78 suggests an additional arm gesture in the middle of the bar, and the hairpin accent—now moved up to the first bb^2—reinforces the heightened urgency.

Pedal for Joining

Chopin sometimes uses the pedal for the opposite purpose. Instead of notating a short pedal to create articulation, a long pedal serves to join structural units together, as in Example 6.12. In this spot most pianists would change the pedal for the new phrase at measure 5, as Chopin's rest seems to suggest. But his pedaling demands the opposite, tying the two phrases together. Note, too, that the *piano* marking comes only at the downbeat, further encouraging the player to link the phrases. The effect is absolutely clear on a nineteenth-century piano, but to create an equally compelling transition between the phrases on a modern instrument, it may help to thin the sound with artful fluttering or half-changes.

Example 6.12. Chopin, Nocturne in E-flat major, op. 9, no. 2, mm. 1–6.

Rhythmic vs. Syncopated pedaling (again)

Chopin—alone among major composers—provides pages and pages of clearly notated pedaling, and virtually all of it follows the *rhythmic* pattern. Example 6.13 is typical, with a pedal change for each bar. Some musicians suggest that Chopin actually practiced syncopated pedaling in the modern way, but was unable to show it in his notation with its inevitable release sign. Had he not felt obliged to supply the release sign—according to this argument—the series of "Ped"s in every measure would convey exactly what modern players always do. But compare measures 41–43 with 35–37. The unusual rests (circled) *demand* rhythmic pedaling; without it the two passages with their contrasting notation would be indistinguishable.

We have already seen the relevance of rhythmic pedaling for Beethoven; it is also the most commonly indicated pattern in the scores of Schumann, Liszt, and Brahms. Although syncopated pedaling gradually became the norm at the modern piano, rhythmic pedaling was evidently still a natural technique for Ignaz Paderewski (1860–1941). In his edition of Chopin's works, some pieces have pedal indications in parentheses where the composer has given none, and the suggestions have all the characteristics of Chopin's own pedaling. (Regrettably, his additions are not always clearly distinguished from what is in the sources—the newer critical editions are much better in this regard.)

I'm not suggesting that we should follow every marking literally—even on Chopin's piano. After all, we aren't trying to replicate some single, ideal

Example 6.13. Chopin, Waltz in A-flat major, op. 34, no. 1, mm. 33–44.

performance. Chopin didn't expect that of his students, either, as this anecdote shows:

> I am entirely indebted to him for the ever-different expression he taught me to obtain in my playing of his works. That is why I so often wept after having worked on one of his pieces which he would then play to me; to show me the style, he would make me hear it in an entirely different way from the previous time. And yet it was wonderful each time![20]

Unfortunately, Chopin will never demonstrate his works for us; we only have the scores. Rhythmic pedaling stares out at us from virtually every page—the least we can do is try!

About the Other Pedal

The Pleyel has an *una corda* pedal, just like a modern piano. Chopin's students described his use of both pedals—separately, together, and in alternation—in a way that suggests he viewed them as a sort of matched set.

> He often coupled them to obtain a soft and veiled sonority, but more often still he would use them separately for brilliant passages, for sustained harmonies, for deep bass notes, and for loud ringing chords.[21]

> Chopin frequently passed, and without transition, from the open to the soft pedal, particularly in enharmonic modulation.[22]

Today's view is quite different: the damper pedal is an indispensable part of the sound virtually everywhere, while the soft pedal is always optional. Perhaps we could come closer to Chopin's mindset by treating the damper pedal—the "loud" pedal—more like the "soft" pedal, as a source of contrast.[23]

Returning to the Modern Piano

The modern piano's power makes it easy to create large shapes using long-range crescendo and diminuendo, and, although very dramatic, this can lead to overlooking the smaller details. One student described her own performance of the C-sharp minor étude, op. 10, no. 4, this way:

In order to express the dramatic character of the piece, I played with driving force, loud volume, and generous use of pedal. However, the light, delicate, and intimate sound of Pleyel convinced me that Chopin would not have appreciated . . . the aggressive, anxious, furious character I created . . .

Her "post-Pleyel" version was much more nuanced, with judicious handling of accents, small swells, slurs, and variety in the texture of the chords.

The distinct registers of the Pleyel helped students appreciate Chopin's skillful use of counterpoint. One wrote:

The Pleyel encouraged me to pay close attention to the balance between parts. The distinctive sounds of the lower, middle, and upper registers made it easier to hear the bass, middle/accompaniment, and melody . . . While the sound of the modern piano is more homogeneous, this quality of listening to all parts simultaneously has helped me to remain more in tune with the shape and direction of each part as well as the dialogue between them.

As we have seen, slow tempi that are beautiful on the modern piano may not work on an instrument with a quicker decay. Students generally enjoyed playing slow music somewhat faster on the Pleyel; the resulting feeling of flow and the lighter texture also led them to employ more *rubato*. This rhythmic freedom made for a more vocal style of performance, with more breathing between phrases. However, the "Pleyel approach" could not simply be transferred to the modern piano. Since each tone takes more time to develop, the tempo must be adjusted, or the music will sound agitated. *Rubato* also needs to be moderated; the larger body of sound creates greater inertia, so the line can't be pushed or pulled too aggressively without sounding unnatural.

The Pleyel is invaluable in making sense of Chopin's pedal markings, but applying those lessons at the Steinway can be challenging. As the examples in this chapter have shown, Chopin delights in the contrast between pedaled and unpedaled sound. Unfortunately, that difference is often too great at the modern piano: the withdrawal of pedal creates an "event" which calls too much attention to itself. As a result, the unpedaled ("dry") sound is rejected altogether, and we lose the possibility of the contrast. But once we understand the effects Chopin was seeking, they can be approximated with partial- or half-pedaling, flutter pedaling, and careful timing of both the onset and release of individual pedal strokes.

You might explore Chopin's ideas about pedaling in two ways. Firstly, begin looking for opportunities to contrast the two modes—pedaled and unpedaled sound. Although you may need to "warm up" the dry bits with subtle touches of pedal, aim for as much contrast as possible. Some examples may seem completely implausible at first, like the passage in Example 6.14:

Example 6.14. Chopin, Ballade no. 4 in F minor, op. 52, mm. 38–46.

The octaves in the left hand, together with the slurred line in the right hand, make this passage nearly unimaginable without pedal. But Chopin has indicated pedaling that points out the four-measure groupings, underlining the fundamental bass progression Gb–Cb–Bb. Try to make the pedal clean and unnoticeable, except at the three spots where it's marked. In those three measures, however, the pedal can be the "main event"—reinforced by your dynamic shaping and use of time.

Secondly, add rhythmic pedaling to your repertoire of pianistic effects. It won't work as naturally or as often as on a nineteenth-century instrument, and it isn't going to replace syncopated pedaling as your default technique. But, as its name suggests, rhythmic pedaling is very good for reinforcing a strong rhythm; dance music is a good place to experiment. Try it with Example 6.15:

Example 6.15. Chopin, *Grande Valse Brillante* in E-flat major, op. 18, mm. 1–12.

Because of the slurs over the barlines in measures 5–7, the right hand sustains while the pedal is released; savor the contrast that comes with the articulation between measure 7 and measure 8. Do you dare play measures 9 and 12 with no pedal?

Notice the two-measure pedal at measures 21–22 (Example 6.16), but don't cheat in the following bars; if the bass notes are smoothly connected, you're not doing it right!

Example 6.16. Chopin, *Grande Valse Brillante* in E-flat major, op. 18, mm. 21–26.

Rhythmic pedaling can also add clarity and definition to textures like Example 6.17.

Example 6.17. Chopin, Prelude in C major, op. 28, no. 1, mm. 1–6.

Rather than changing the pedal with each bass note and producing a legato bass line, try releasing the pedal with the last note of each bar, just as the score says. Enjoy the breath that Chopin places between the harmonies. If the gap sounds too big, hold the last note of the measure a fraction longer.

In Conclusion

Chopin is a composer we think we know well. Pianists who find his style more accessible than that of the classical composers may be tempted to just do "what comes naturally." But old recordings make it clear that "our" Chopin is actually a recent style. Koczalski, de Pachmann, Paderewski, Cortot: all were born in the nineteenth century, and studied with students or contemporaries of Chopin. Their idiosyncratic playing—full of extravagant rubato, unsynchronized hands, and extreme tempi—sounds strange now, sometimes shocking. Even their pianos, though not from Chopin's day, don't quite resemble current Steinways. Fascinating for performers, these recordings have now become the subject of scholarly research.[24]

Our interpretations are bound to be influenced by the times we live in; no piano will bring us back to the world of Chopin and his contemporaries. Yet careful study of Chopin's notation with the characteristics of his piano in mind can reveal the effects he sought, even if we will never reproduce them. There is certainly no "right" way to play anything, perhaps especially Chopin's highly individual music. But a fresh reading of the scores, colored by a vivid image of Chopin at the Pleyel in his Parisian salon, can stimulate our imaginations and expand our creativity.

Chapter Seven

The Clavichord

Last but Not Least . . .

This is a book about pianos and piano-playing, so I didn't feature the clavichord at the beginning—even if that's where it belongs chronologically. But because of its crucial role in my own thinking and because it made such a big impression on the students in the seminar, I couldn't leave it out, either.

Today the clavichord seems exotic, but in eighteenth-century Germany it was the most common of all keyboard instruments, known by the generic term *Clavier* ("keyboard"). It was also the least expensive, since the case is just a rectangular box and the only moving parts are the keys themselves. Figure 7.1 shows how it works, and the website https://boydellandbrewer.com/piano-playing-revisited-hb.html includes several clips relating to the clavichord. There are no dampers for the strings. Instead, a long strip of cloth ("listing") prevents them from vibrating until a key is depressed, when the tangent (a piece of brass attached to the end of the key opposite the player's

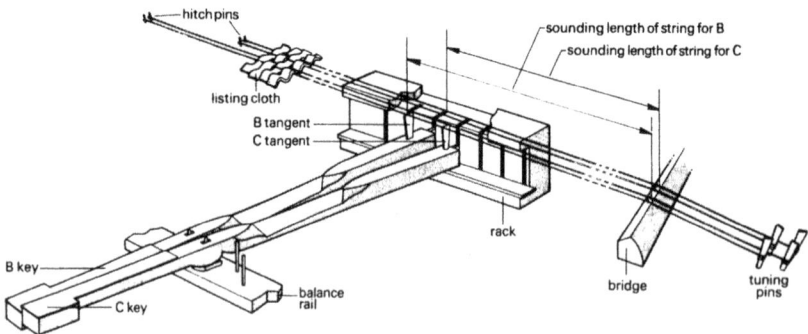

Figure 7.1. Clavichord action, showing two keys, from *New Grove*, "Clavichord."

finger) divides the corresponding strings (usually two per unison) into two segments. Then the *sounding length* (the segment from the tangent to the bridge), energized by the tangent, is free to vibrate until the key is released, when the cloth again damps the entire string.

Despite the elegance and simplicity of its design, the clavichord can be frustratingly difficult to play, since every irregularity in touch is immediately audible (I call it a lie detector). Two approaches to the key that make similar sounds on a piano may produce totally different effects on the clavichord, one beautiful and the next unacceptable. It is also impractical for concerts, since its loudest sound scarcely compares with a modern instrument's *mezzo piano*, although its ability to play extremely softly still gives it a wide dynamic range. But along with these liabilities come certain advantages: modulating the pressure on a key affects the sustain of a note, or its pitch, and can even create a vibrato (*Bebung*). C. P. E. Bach's remark that a good clavichordist makes an accomplished harpsichordist, but not the reverse, becomes easy to understand after a few minutes' acquaintance with the instrument.

Here's how the seminar students described their work at the clavichord:

- "it's like a meditation—you have to go slowly and concentrate on staying perfectly centered"
- "it requires you to stay in the moment; you can't let your attention jump ahead or lag behind"
- "I learned to remain present with each gesture, with each note as it unfolds"
- "if I don't keep track of each of the voices, then the notes don't sound"
- "I love feeling the vibrations in the key itself—you realize you're connected to the strings"
- "when I played the piano after working at the clavichord, I was aware of the movement of the hammers"
- "turning to the grand piano after playing the clavichord for an hour, my hand felt—I don't know how to describe it—*activated*"

C. P. E. Bach's *empfindsamer Stil* (sensitive style) works best on the clavichord, his favorite instrument; its intimate dynamics and expressive *Bebung* are also central to the works of lesser-known composers such as Johann Gottfried Müthel (1728–1788) and Ernst Wilhelm Wolf (1735–1792). For musicians interested in this repertoire, the clavichord is truly indispensable. It has also found another, more modern home: Oscar Peterson, Keith Jarrett, and Friedrich Gulda have all made persuasive recordings of jazz on clavichord. But it was for insight into the works of J. S. Bach that I included it in the seminar.

J. S. Bach is still considered an essential part of a pianist's training. His music has been called "indestructible" because the pieces can work with nearly any tempo or dynamic scheme, and a touch ranging from extreme staccato to extreme legato. Lots of pedal, no pedal; terraced dynamics, no dynamics—this repertoire has been played in so many ways that settling on an interpretation and performing with conviction can be a real challenge. Some pianists have looked to the harpsichord for guidance, restricting themselves to the tools available at that instrument. Following this strategy, the pedal is off-limits, dynamics must mimic the registral effects of the harpsichord, and small-scale inflections are made only by varying the note lengths (agogics) and articulation. I find the results of this generally unsatisfactory: the sound is unattractive, and an overuse of agogic accent disturbs the rhythm. Others take a different approach: instead of employing harpsichord tactics at the piano, they try to imitate the sound of the harpsichord by using a short, sharp staccato touch. Although used to great effect by Glenn Gould, this technique can quickly degenerate into mannerism, and isn't conducive to the *cantabile* that Bach advocates (more on that below).

Since the clavichord—like the piano—is a touch-sensitive instrument (i.e., the force applied to the key controls the dynamic level), I prefer to view the piano as a very loud clavichord and seek inspiration there, rather than from the harpsichord. Its relevance for Bach performance is indisputable. It was ubiquitous at the time and was used for performances in the Bach household. J. S. Bach's early biographer Forkel even claimed that it was Sebastian's favorite instrument, as well as Carl Philipp's. And since many of the strategies that the clavichord requires—above all, a precisely balanced support of the arm behind each finger stroke—are also appropriate at the piano, the clavichord can be a wonderful tool for developing technique.

For my own understanding of the clavichord, I am deeply indebted to Joel Speerstra, with whom I spent many rewarding hours at the instrument. In his book, *J. S. Bach and the Pedal Clavichord*, Speerstra leans heavily on an account of Bach's keyboard technique by Friedrich Konrad Griepenkerl that appeared in the preface to his 1820 edition of the Chromatic Fantasy. Although Griepenkerl never observed Bach's playing first-hand, and his description is confusing in places, I was struck by one casual, off-hand comment: his assertion that the clavichord "is far better for training the hand [than the piano]. Transferring to the piano [the technique learned at the clavichord] really presents no difficulties, since the touch remains the same and the forte-piano only allows greater carelessness . . ."[1]

Griepenkerl was writing about the pianos of 1820; I'm not sure he would make the same claim for today's Steinway with its far greater touch-weight and key dip. But the clavichord's most valuable lessons do not depend on how far the key travels or how much force it takes to press it down, but rather on what happens after the sound has been produced.

The piano's sound is determined by the velocity of the hammer when it reaches the string, but the player is only in control until the moment of escapement (the slight resistance we feel about two-thirds of the way through the key's descent). For the remainder of the keystroke (the "follow-through"), the hammer is in free flight and the pianist's movements no longer influence its trajectory, although they certainly determine how one note leads to the next. The tangent of the clavichord, however, is always directly connected to the player's finger, so every action of the player—even during the follow-through—is audible.

A student described this perfectly:

> [I]f one fails to maintain a certain pressure [on the key] after the attack, the tangent bounces off the string, cutting off the sound, whose resonance depends on the tangent remaining in contact with the string for the full duration of the note . . . The clavichord is unequivocal: a good follow-through produces a clear, vibrant sound; if the follow-through is deficient, the sound dies immediately. It's much easier to discern than on a modern piano, where even a thoughtless follow-through still produces a normal sound from the instrument. The clavichord helped me practice this gesture, and that's why I wish I had access to one more regularly. The slower, well-supported follow-through demanded by the clavichord, when transferred to the modern piano, helps tremendously in the development of a rich, connected, projecting sound.

Familiar technical injunctions like "play into the keys" or "play to the bottom of the keys" have a greater impact at the clavichord, where the player actually raises and bends the string at the end of the stroke. The string tension and vibration can be felt through the key, and the success or failure of the tone production provides audible feedback. Even *watching* the tangent contact the string is instructive, since it functions as a direct extension of the player's fingertip.

Some clavichords with very low string tension (either very small ones, or many of the "revival" instruments popular in England in the 1950s and 60s) respond well to a pure finger technique. But the heavier stringing of eighteenth-century German instruments requires more support than can be provided by an individual finger (especially one of the weaker fingers). Producing a clear sound on every note requires a careful choreography of the hand and arm,[2] and Speerstra relates these movements to the doctrine of *"Musica Poetica"* or *musical figures*, developed by seventeenth-century German theorists. The short outline of *Musica Poetica* given here scarcely does justice to Speerstra's elegant treatment of the subject.

Musica Poetica: At the Intersection of Improvisation and Keyboard Technique

Bach's young students were trained not only to play and sing but also to improvise and to compose. They began by learning to play short musical figures like those in Figure 7.2 with a single gesture of the arm. These figures, the "words" of the baroque musical language, became the raw material of improvisation and composition. And since they were associated with physical gestures, they also formed the foundation of keyboard technique. Variations of these figures were practiced across the keyboard, and ultimately combined to form pieces; Bach's Two-Part Inventions were models of how this could be done.

Figure 7.2 is taken from Speerstra's book; the calligraphic interpretations are also his.[3]

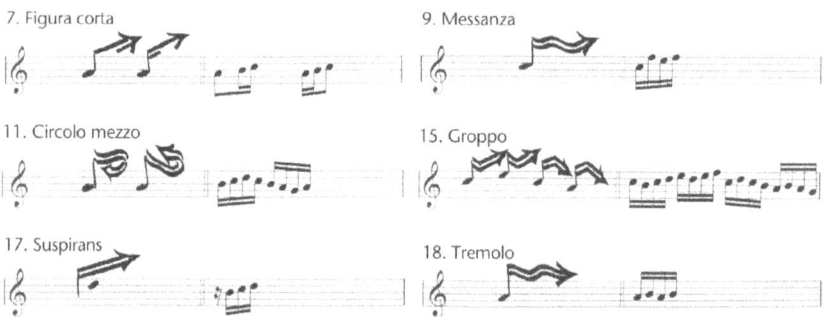

Figure 7.2. Sample figures of *Musica Poetica*, from Speerstra, *J. S. Bach and the Pedal Clavichord.*

For Bach's young beginners, this all-encompassing system may have made music as natural as talking or breathing. But for my students, struggling to make consistent sounds at the clavichord, it was just a simple way to break longer passages into small units that made both musical and technical sense. Working on each shape individually kept them "in the moment," and helped them find suitable arm movements, as well as the necessary balance between suppleness and firmness in the hand.

Elements of Performance

Touch and Articulation

Most of the students approached Bach at the piano with a primarily legato touch. Some pointed to Bach's own preface to the Inventions, where he advocates a *cantabile* style:

> An Honest Guide, by which the lovers of the *Clavier*, particularly those who desire to learn, are shown a plain way, not only (1) to learn to play neatly in two parts, but also, with further *progress*, (2) to play correctly and well in three *obbligato parts*; and, at the same time, not only to obtain good musical *themes*, but also to develop them well; above all, however, to achieve a *cantabile style of playing*, and along with it, to gain a strong foretaste of *composition*.

However, it may be a mistake to equate Bach's *cantabile* (= "singing") with *our* notion of beautiful singing—*bel canto*—a legato-based ideal derived from nineteenth-century Italian opera. Since consonants figure prominently in sung German, Bach's vocal ideal might correspond to a highly articulated style at the keyboard. The instrumental music of Bach's predecessors is also consistent with this hypothesis. In the seventeenth century, the default articulation for string players was a separate bow stroke for each note—even for the individual notes of quick, written-out trills—and wind players were also accustomed to tonguing every note.[4] Legato was used for small ornaments of two to eight notes, just like melismatic figuration in vocal music or the individual figures of *Musica Poetica*. In other words, keyboard players using their fingers to articulate small groups of notes are doing just what singers do when they pronounce individual words, or string players when they organize their bow strokes.

Slurs are rarely indicated in baroque music, since the figures of *Musica Poetica* implicitly connect notes ornamenting a single pitch or interval. Because the figures typically express a single harmony and rarely straddle

Example 7.1. J. S. Bach, Invention no. 8 in F major, BWV 779, mm. 1–3, 8–9.

barlines or even beats, the resulting articulation patterns line up with the meter and clarify the harmonic rhythm. But when I ask students to subdivide the phrases in a piece by Bach, they usually organize the figuration as a series of upbeats, as in the opening of Invention 8 (Example 7.1). They treat the main notes of the figuration as goals and put them at the *ends* of their groups, while the baroque figures ordinarily *begin* with the principal note. Harmony changes no longer coincide with the groupings, but arrive instead on the final note of a group, as in measure 8 of the example.

The students readily agreed that "their" groupings could not be performed literally, since the breaks produce accents in the wrong places. This didn't matter to them because the grouping was purely theoretical; the individual units would be connected by a continuous legato in performance. Nevertheless, a series of slurs of varied lengths that sounds completely natural at the clavichord or harpsichord produces quite a different effect at the piano: fussy and choppy. The piano really does demand a smoother surface.

Ultimately, the students were able to convey the gestures developed at the clavichord with a more "pianistic" touch. Instead of trying to separate the individual figures, I asked them to make sure the *function* of each note within a figure was clear in their performance (whether metrically strong or weak, dissonant or consonant, marking a new harmony or change of direction, serving only as a passing/neighbor tone). This approach, like fluent speech, revealed the music's sense without cutting it into small segments.

Clavichords and touch: a further twist
There are two types of clavichords, *fretted* and *unfretted*; the students whose experiences are described in this chapter worked with an *unfretted* example. On fretted clavichords, certain pairs of notes, such as (typically) C–C♯, E♭–E, F–F♯, G–G♯, B♭–B, share the same strings, and consequently can't be played simultaneously. The tangents of these adjacent keys produce different pitches by stopping the strings at a different point, just like a violinist's fingers. To play two such notes in a descending succession, the higher note must be released for a fraction of a second, otherwise the lower note will not sound. Evidently this was not considered a serious drawback, since fretted clavichords were common in Germany well into the second half of the eighteenth century (a fretted clavichord by Stein accompanied the Mozart family on their travels during Wolfgang's childhood). I consider this additional evidence for a prevailing (slightly) non-legato touch, even on the fortepiano.

Tempo

The clavichord has a moderating effect on tempo. Its relatively short sustain precludes very slow tempi (e.g., Richter's performance of the C-sharp minor fugue from Book I of the *Well-Tempered Clavier* at $\downarrow$ = 38), while playing too quickly prevents individual notes from speaking and makes detailed articulation impossible. But a tempo determined at the clavichord may reveal the music's character in a way that can be transferred to the piano, even if the speed changes.

Register

Most of Bach's keyboard music uses only C–c^3, with the occasional BB or d^3. From the modern pianist's perspective, this is an extremely conservative range. At the clavichord, however, the contrast within these four octaves is very dramatic. Each register even demands its own technique; the stiff, short strings in the treble pose different challenges from the long, flexible bass strings. The use of different technical approaches for different registers may seem strange to a pianist, but it is certainly familiar to any singer, or indeed to the players of most other instruments. The sounds themselves are also very different: the bass generally full and round, the treble extremely delicate and silvery. In many pieces Bach deploys the registers just as strategically as Beethoven, albeit on a smaller scale. But because Bach's extremes are nowhere near the limits of the modern piano, it's easy to overlook his design; careful attention to register can enliven even the simplest pieces.

Consider the first prelude and fugue from the *Well-Tempered Clavier*. Each begins with middle C sounded alone. The prelude starts with the hands very close together, spanning the tenth c^1–e^2. Bach gradually expands upwards, reaching a^2 in the fifth bar; the piece then moves inexorably downwards, eventually settling into the range of G–g^1 for the extended pedal point (mm. 24–31). The arrival of the tonic in measure 32 is intensified by the low CC— the first appearance of that register—and the physicality of settling deeply[5] into that note, then repeating it for four bars until the end of the piece, is truly satisfying. The fugue, on the other hand, never uses the bottom of the keyboard, and ends with a (heavenward?) ascent to c^3, in perfect contrast to the (earthbound?) grounding at the end of the prelude.

The D major Toccata (Example 7.2) uses register in another way:

Example 7.2. J. S. Bach, Toccata in D major, BWV 912, mm. 1–6.

Here there is nothing *but* register contrast! The five-fold repetition of the opening material, covering virtually the entire keyboard, depends for its interest on the color changes that any eighteenth-century instrument would have displayed. At the modern piano, this passage makes little sense unless the player imaginatively and skillfully conveys the same drama within these three-and-a-half octaves, now situated comfortably in the middle of the piano's vastly broader compass. The subsequent passage beginning at measure 11 is similar, but with an ascending pattern (and only four repetitions).

Polyphony

Much of Bach's keyboard music features three- and four-part polyphony, and many pianists delight in bringing out particular voices—especially fugal entries, but also various counter-subjects and anything else that captures their interest. On the piano, this is often the easiest way to create an attractive, intelligible texture. On the harpsichord, however, this kind of voicing isn't possible, and on the clavichord it isn't necessary. Instead, as in good chamber music or ensemble singing, the historical instruments project each line distinctly because of the register effects described above. As the Toccata example suggests, simply moving up or down by a fourth or fifth is enough to create a fresh color; polyphony that would be vibrant and clear on a harpsichord or clavichord can sound muddy and confusing on the piano without active intervention on the part of the player.

Understanding the nature of the problem suggests a different solution at the piano: instead of "dumbing down" the music and forcing the listener to follow a single foregrounded line, one can strive for the *impression* of equal voices. This requires very careful balancing of the parts, along with clear shaping of the individual lines, but can produce a richer result. We have already encountered this topic (see the discussion in connection with Mozart on p. 31, and Chopin on p. 134), but since baroque music is more strictly polyphonic than later styles, it is even more important here. Simultaneous independent lines are the essence of this style, and the modern piano's propensity to sing by featuring a single voice against an accompaniment in the background can be a real hindrance. The challenge is to give every line its due.

A Broader Context for Baroque Keyboard Music

There is a lot to learn from the clavichord, and, for a keyboard player, there is nothing like putting your own hands on one and exploring its special, intimate world for yourself. The harpsichord, too, has a lot to teach us. But if we could visit Bach's world we would find more than a different set of instruments: we would encounter an entirely different set of expectations. Bach's students and colleagues were able to improvise pieces and compose them; they could realize a bass line with or without figures to accompany different kinds of ensembles; they could play for dancers, or improvise music for a church service. We cannot know how these skills affected their solo performances. But since many baroque pieces resemble composed-out realizations of a bass, eighteenth-century players who were trained in composition and improvisation—like today's jazz musicians—might have treated such scores as little more than a framework, playing with much more freedom than we ever hear today.

Bach was singled out for criticism because he notated ornamentation and other details that his contemporaries usually left to the discretion of the performer. That's fortunate for today's players who lack the necessary training to add these on their own. But if we're serious about Bach's music, shouldn't we be attempting to recover the skills that he expected from his students, like accompaniment from a bass line, improvisation on chorale melodies, and the invention of simple pieces? Those topics are certainly beyond the scope of this book, but they needn't be beyond the aspirations of today's creative musicians.

Epilogue

Creativity in the Performance of Old Music

Period instruments and contemporary written accounts can illuminate the nuts and bolts of piano playing: dynamics, note lengths, articulation, voicing, pedaling. But what about creativity? By learning how the music was played in the past, do we give up the freedom to create in the present? One of the seminar students struggled poignantly to express this dilemma:

> What is tasteful or appropriate for a style of music always seems to be in direct conflict with the personality or ego of the performer . . . Is it our responsibility to accurately interpret the music as intended by the composer at the moment of conception or should we be trying to breathe new life into this music? We have witnessed in the last century a trend toward self-indulgent interpretations of music without careful adherence to the stylistic intricacies that make one composer's works distinguishable from another's. These details are often sacrificed, as a result of a lack of knowledge or neglect, for what sounds pleasing on the modern instrument. . . . Are we then just a vessel for the composer's ideas or do we play an even greater role in the creation of this music? To what extent can the performer take personal liberties with the music and still stay true to the spirit of a work?

"Accurately interpret" vs. "take personal liberties." Be a "vessel" or be "self-indulgent." Are these the only alternatives? The dilemma is quite recent, since the objective conception of performance (performer as "vessel") arose only after the First World War. Its proponents believed that the player should offer "just the facts, ma'am;" anything more only reflects the arrogance of the performer's ego. Stravinsky makes the point forcefully:

The sin against the spirit of the work always begins with a sin against its letter and leads to the endless follies which an ever-flourishing literature in the worst taste does its best to sanction. Thus it follows that a *crescendo*, as we all know, is always accompanied by a speeding up of movement, while a slowing down never fails to accompany a *diminuendo*. The superfluous is refined upon; a *piano, piano pianissimo* is delicately sought after; great pride is taken in perfecting useless nuances—a concern that usually goes hand in hand with inaccurate rhythm . . .[1]

An equally clear statement of the older, opposite view can be found in Louis Spohr's *Violinschule* of 1832, which distinguishes between a (merely) "correct style," marked by minute observance of all the composer's indications, and a "fine style," which requires the performer to make "additions of his own"; these include "the accentuation and separation of musical phrases" and the "accelerating" and "slackening" of the time, according to the character of a passage.[2]

In his disdain for that "fine style," Stravinsky reserved his most acerbic remarks for the conductor: "Perched on his sibylline tripod, he imposes his own movements, his own particular shadings upon the compositions he conducts, and he even reaches the point of talking with a naïve impudence of his specialities, of *his* fifth, of *his* seventh, the way a chef boasts of a dish of his own concoction."[3]

The new approach succeeded in banishing many of the extremes of interpretive license that can still be heard on early twentieth-century recordings. Perhaps that was a good thing (I'm not so sure); but it also led to a "sanitized" kind of performance in which music lost some of its essential vitality and expressivity. The student quoted at the head of this chapter fears that the historical approach demands even more objectivity, that "interpreting accurately" precludes "breathing new life into the music."

Musicians are not alone in their struggles with historical texts and past practices. In "Law, Music and other Performing Arts," a review of Nicholas Kenyon's essay collection *Authenticity and Early Music*, the lawyers (and amateur musicians) Sanford Levinson and J. M. Balkin argue that their colleagues could learn something about the current state of the legal profession from the early music movement.

It is our thesis that the early-music movement is best understood as attempting what the English historian Eric Hobsbawm calls the "invention of tradition." Hobsbawm defines "invented traditions" as "responses to novel situations which take the form of reference to old situations, or which establish their own past by quasi-obligatory repetition." Faced with "the constant change and innovation of the modern world," one engages in an "attempt to structure at least some parts of social life within it as unchanging and invariant."[4]

Levinson and Balkin are concerned with the anxiety of modernity, which they describe as "the increasing sense of isolation and estrangement from the past and from tradition spurred on by constantly accelerating changes in culture, economy, and technology."[5] This anxiety can lead to rigidity, and this rigidity—both in the law and in music—is the target of their argument. But if, as Levinson and Balkin suggest, "historical" performers are guilty of responding to modernist anxiety with Hobsbawm's scornful "reference to old situations" (i.e., by adopting old instruments and studying old performance treatises), then surely "conventional" performers are dealing with the same anxiety by his "quasi-obligatory repetition" (i.e., concerts of canonical works performed in a canonical fashion).

Levinson and Balkin see themselves as pragmatists, and view the law as a living, flexible system in which old statutes or legal precedents should be applied imaginatively to modern situations. The opposite position is "originalism," a legal philosophy that seeks to restrict interpretation to the original intent of a law's authors—typically in the service of extremely conservative positions, not unlike religious fundamentalism. Their article asserts that a concern with fidelity to composers' intentions is a sort of musical originalism or fundamentalism. Performers of music, who are obliged to execute the "commands" of composers, are compared with lawyers and judges—"performers of the law"—who are obliged to execute the "commands" of legislators. For both kinds of performers, anxious rigidity is a liability that prevents them from adapting to current conditions. As a corrective, Levinson and Balkin propose a flexible view of tradition, neatly summarized at the conclusion of their essay: "Tradition, like history, is something that is continually being recreated and remodeled in the present, even as it is represented as something fixed and unchangeable."[6]

This is definitely "breathing new life" into something old, and they see the notion of authenticity, as used in the book under review, as its opposite. It's not hard to see why: proponents of "musical authenticity" explicitly reject certain aspects of performance that had been "remodeled in the present," including modern instruments. But since the publication of those essays in 1988, the term "authenticity" has been thoroughly discredited in musical circles, thanks largely to polemical articles by Richard Taruskin, beginning with his contribution to the very volume under review.[7] Early promoters of early music used the idea of authenticity to make claims that are easy to ridicule, like advertising a radio broadcast as "Bach's Mass as Bach himself heard it" (we should blame the publicists, not the musicians). Will Crutchfield, in his contribution to the book,[8] reminds us that "authenticity" has another meaning in the context of performance, and Balkin and Levinson make this the culmination of their argument. Here they quote Crutchfield extensively, with their own commentary:

> "This authenticity is what the standee at the opera means when he says he has heard 'the real thing,' 'the genuine article.'" When a performance is authentic in the sense of genuineness, "we feel the music and musician are one . . . The Irish theologian William Fitzgerald supplied . . . the right citation for this: 'That is called Authentic, which is sufficient unto itself, which commends, sustains, proves itself, and hath credit and authority from itself.'"
>
> The notion of authenticity as genuineness is deeply tied to the concept of tradition and one's relation to the past. The authentic performance is immersed in a tradition, so that the tradition springs from within it unself-consciously; it is the living embodiment of tradition, of the past. That is why it is sufficient to itself, and needs authority from no outside source. Hence another meaning of "authentic" is idiomatic, sincere, and unaffected. Nevertheless, this conception of authenticity leads to what we might call the "paradox of authenticity." The more one self-consciously tries to be authentic to a tradition, the less authentic one's practice becomes; conversely, true authenticity always emerges where one least expects it, and indeed, it emerges virtually without any effort on the part of the actors who are enmeshed in authentic practice.[9]

To be "enmeshed in authentic practice"—caught, but not trapped; constrained, but creative—in the pursuit of performances that are "idiomatic, sincere, and unaffected"—who could wish for more?

The "authentic practice" of eighteenth-century musicians like Türk and C. P. E. Bach had nothing in common with the kind of objective performance praised by Stravinsky, or with the originalism decried by Balkin and Levinson. Here is Türk's description of a good performer:

> Whoever performs a composition so that the affect (character, etc.), even in every single passage, is most faithfully expressed, and that the tones become at the same time a language of feelings, of this person it is said that he is a good executant. Good execution [or 'performance': his German term is *Vortrag*], therefore, is the most important, but at the same time, the most difficult task of making music.[10]

He then provides forty pages of advice for the subtle manipulation of rhythm, articulation, and dynamics: Stravinsky's "useless nuances." But this time they don't originate with self-aggrandizing conductors of the twentieth century, or with the nineteenth-century romanticizing editors we encountered in Chapter 2. Instead we get the keys to eighteenth-century style as it was understood by the best practitioners at the time. Today's students may see these essential elements of interpretation as "personal liberties," but for Türk, "faithfulness" *is* "breathing life into the music," and it doesn't happen just by slavishly playing what's printed. He has no use for the "accurate" type of performer: "For even with all his facility in reading notes and in playing, he will never attain his main purpose, which is to move the heart of his listener, without good execution."[11] C. P. E. Bach agrees:

> More often than not, one meets technicians, nimble keyboardists by profession, who . . . astound us with their prowess without ever touching our sensibilities. They overwhelm our hearing without satisfying it and stun the mind without moving it. . . . What comprises good performance? The ability through singing or playing to make the ear conscious of the true content and affect [emotional content] of a composition.

He goes on to explain that "The subject matter of performance [i.e., what he will teach in his book] is the loudness and softness of tones, touch, the snap [a quick trill], legato and staccato execution, the vibrato [on the clavichord], arpeggiation, the holding of tones, the retard and accelerando."[12]

The objective view confuses the score with the music, and asserts that whatever is not in the score does not belong in the performance. Bach and Türk had a far broader conception of the performer's role, believing that good performance depends on something that cannot be read directly from the score—namely the "true content and affect of a composition"—and requires subtleties that are also not notated ("the loudness and softness . . . the holding of tones, the retard and accelerando").

This perspective already grants a performer more freedom than the twentieth-century one expressed by Stravinsky. But why not treat the challenge of "interpreting accurately" (i.e., historically) as a source of inspiration *in itself* rather than a limitation? Stravinsky himself recognizes the value of constraints in the creative process:

> My freedom will be so much the greater and more meaningful the more I surround myself with obstacles. Whatever diminishes constraint diminishes

strength. The more constraints one imposes, the more one frees one's self of the chains that shackle the spirit.[13]

He is particularly sensitive to the uses of history, presumably defending his own neo-classical works: "My own experience has long convinced me that any historical fact, recent or distant, may well be utilized as a stimulus to set the creative faculty in motion, but never as an aid for clearing up difficulties."[14]

It's not entirely clear what he means by "an aid for clearing up difficulties"; perhaps he is worried about historical facts being used to justify the interpretive practices of which he disapproves—the "ever-flourishing literature in the worst taste." (I wish I knew exactly which literature he had in mind!) For myself, I am just as delighted by historical facts that "clear up difficulties" as by those that provide a stimulus for the creative faculty. Historical instruments also appeal to me for the same reasons: the problems they are able to solve, and the compelling performances they can inspire.

Of course, there are bad performances on historical instruments and great ones on modern instruments. But much of today's music-making is marred by a deep *fear of interpreting*, with bland, dutiful-sounding results. That fear has (at least) two sources: the perceived need for a perfectly smooth surface, and a deep anxiety about performing "correctly." Together these factors inhibit creativity, producing unduly cautious and uninflected playing instead of the communicative and individually stamped performances that I crave.

By now you know where I stand; this entire book can be summarized as a response to those concerns. To the first one, I say this: Just because the modern piano can produce a more continuous, smooth surface than any of the earlier instruments does not mean that one has to play it that way—all the time. The piano is remarkably versatile; the sounds it can produce are limited primarily by our imagination. And to feed that imagination, the scores themselves are filled with suggestions once we know how to read them.

As for the second, more fundamental problem: The performances I admire exude *authority*, not correctness. Striving to understand the composers' intentions isn't a moral obligation, a way to avoid "errors," but rather a path towards ownership of the material. With ownership comes conviction, and the rewards of conviction are confidence and freedom—real authenticity, the genuine article!

Appendix

Overtone Structure of the Steinway and Walter, Compared

The following graphs show the distribution of upper partials in the different registers of a Steinway and of a Walter copy, made with the "Pianalyzer" function of the Reyburn Cybertuner software. The left column (P#) indicates the partial: 1 is the fundamental, 2 is the octave above, 3 is the twelfth, etc. The values for "Volume Units" are also represented by the horizontal bars. From the "Sustain seconds" column we can see that for both pianos the higher the partial is, the quicker the decay.

On the Steinway, the fundamental and the first harmonic (= second partial) account for most of the sound. On the fortepiano, both the second and fourth partials (one and two octaves above the fundamental), are stronger than the fundamental, and all the partials up to the tenth make up a significant proportion of the sound. This helps explain why the added resonance provided by the pedal is more noticeable on the modern instrument. The first graphs (Figures A.1 and A.2) show middle C (c^1).

The next graphs (Figures A.3 and A.4) show c^2 and c^3 on the Steinway (C5 and C6 in the Pianalyzer notation). The highest partials have disappeared (they are too high to be audible), but the basic shape remains consistent with c^1: the fundamental is by far the strongest component of the sound.

On the Walter, however, each octave is quite distinctive (Figures A.5 and A.6). c^2 has almost equal contributions from the second, third, and fourth partials, while c^3 is characterized by a very strong second partial.

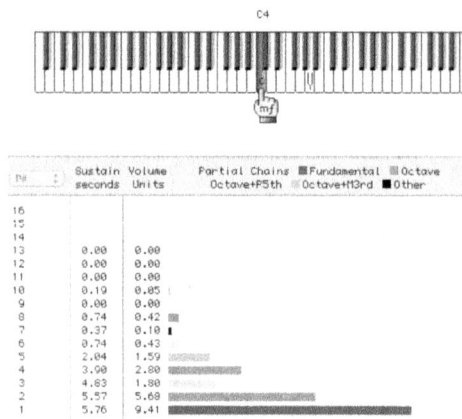

Figure A.1. c^1 (C4 in the Pianalyzer notation) on the Steinway.

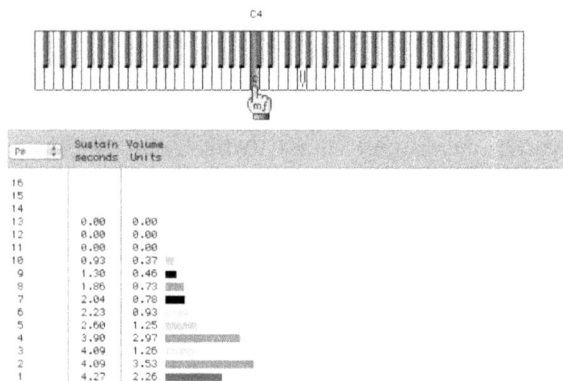

Figure A.2. c^1 (C4) on the Walter.

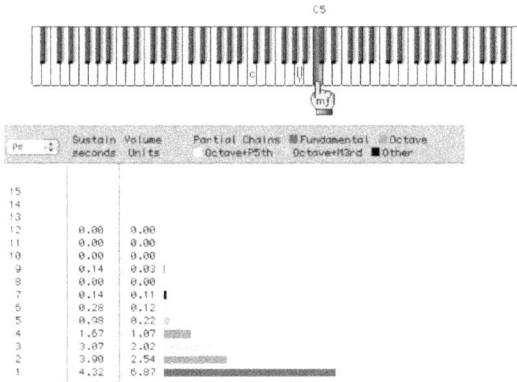

Figure A.3. c^2 (C5) on the Steinway.

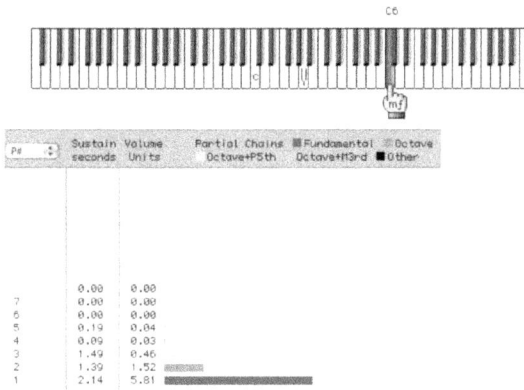

Figure A.4. c^3 (C6) on the Steinway.

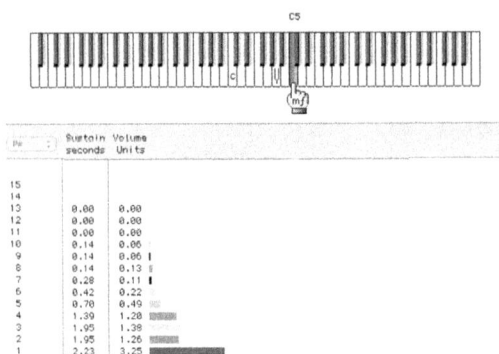

Figure A.5. c^2 (C5) on the Walter.

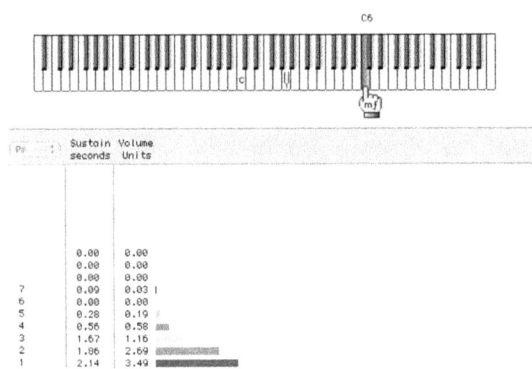

Figure A.6. c^3 (C6) on the Walter.

Glossary of Terms

Articulation:	The clear onset of a tone, and its separation from the previous tone. Can also refer to the specific manner of attacking and releasing tones.
Attack (part of piano sound):	The first part of the sound after the hammer hits the strings. *See also:* Sustain, Decay.
Damping:	The effect of lowering the damper(s) onto a piano's strings, either by releasing a key or the pedal.
Decay (part of piano sound):	The "tail" of the piano's sound, as it fades away.
Finger-pedal (overholding):	Holding down notes (typically chord tones) with the fingers for longer than their written value, for an effect that is more typically produced by means of the pedal. Other (more formal) terms are "prolonged touch," *legatissimo*, over-legato.
Fortepiano:	Commonly used to refer to historical pianos in general, or to late eighteenth-century types in particular.
Historical Performance:	An approach to musical interpretation that seeks to understand a composer's expectations in the light of historical information. These include the precise meaning of the written symbols, the instrument to be used, the likely performance venue, etc.
Key-dip:	The distance traveled by the front of the key when depressed: .04" on a Steinway grand, less on earlier pianos.
Legato pedaling:	*See* Syncopated pedaling.
Moderator (pedal):	On early pianos, a device that introduces a strip of cloth between the hammer and the string, producing a muffled sound.

Ordinary touch:	According to eighteenth-century writers, the "ordinary" (German: *ordentliche* or *gewöhnliche*) way of playing, neither staccato nor legato, which did not require any special sign or indication.
Piano:	General term for any keyboard instrument with hammers, from Cristofori's to the Steinway.
Rhythmic pedaling:	Style of pedaling where the pedal is depressed (or the knee-lever is raised) simultaneously with the bass note. *Compare* Syncopated pedaling.
Romantic piano:	A piano from the nineteenth century, later than a classic fortepiano, but not yet a modern piano.
Slur:	A curved line over two or more notes. These notes are connected to each other, and are distinct from what precedes and follows. According to eighteenth-century sources, the first note under the slur should be emphasized, followed by diminuendo; the last note was to be played lightly and shortened. When a slur appears over an arpeggiated accompaniment, finger-pedal (overholding) is expected. In the nineteenth century, as legato became the norm, (longer) curved lines indicated phrasing instead of articulation.
Stroke (articulation mark):	A vertical line or, more commonly in engraved music, a wedge shape used to designate staccato. According to some writers, it is interchangeable with the dot, while others assert that the stroke is shorter or stronger.
Sustain (part of piano sound):	The singing part of the tone, after the initial attack.
Syncopated pedaling:	Style of pedaling where the pedal or knee-lever is *released* simultaneously with the bass note, and then immediately redeployed. It is also known as legato pedaling. *Compare* Rhythmic Pedaling
Texture:	The relationship among the sounds heard simultaneously, e.g., chords, counterpoint, melody and accompaniment. The basic texture is set by the composer, but by controlling the prominence of each element, the player determines whether the result is thick or thin, simple or complex.

Touch:

Used in several distinct senses: 1. Referring to the length of notes (legato, staccato, ordinary touch); 2. Referring to the energy the player imparts to the key (strong or weak touch); 3. Referring to the mechanical setup of a keyboard (shallow or deep; heavy or light).

Treatise:

An instructional book. As used here, the comprehensive guides to performance by C. P. E. Bach and his contemporaries.

Wedge:

See Stroke.

Notes

Preface

1. Professor Saulnier was an invaluable partner. His own enthusiasm for the Pleyel—he had recorded a beautiful all-Chopin CD on it—set the tone for the class; it wouldn't have worked without him. All sixteen students earned my gratitude for their unflagging enthusiasm and commitment: Vincent Béland-Bernard, Michel-Alexandre Broekaert, Patrick Cashin, Eunice Chen, Carol-Anne Fraser, Jean-Simon Gaudreau, Julio Gonzalo, Junghwa Hong, Alison Kilgannon, Jonathan Kilgannon, Ryan Kolodziej, Simon Larivière, Jean-François Latour, Sofia Mycyk, Elizabeth Schumann, and Marie-Hélène Trempe.

Chapter One

1. Of course there are differences among the different manufacturers, just as there are differences among individual instruments of the same make. But for the purposes of this book, all "modern" pianos are sufficiently alike to be discussed together.
2. Eigeldinger, *Chopin*, 26. This book is a treasure trove for anyone who plays Chopin. It contains accounts of Chopin's playing and his teaching organized by topic (i.e., technique, or *rubato)*, with an index that allows one to easily find remarks pertaining to a particular piece.
3. C. P. E. Bach, *Essay*, 37.
4. This Schirmer edition is still available, and appears to be based on a series of "Instructive Editions" of classical works prepared by Sigmund Lebert and published in Stuttgart in 1871–90.
5. *Toronto Globe and Mail* interview with Robert Everett-Green, "Does he have the right stuff?" March 8, 2000. Accessed May 7, 2018 at https://www.theglobeandmail.com/arts/does-he-have-the-right-stuff/article18421452/.
6. Harnoncourt, *Baroque Music Today*, 17.

Chapter Two

1. Harnoncourt, *Baroque Music Today*, 39.
2. See Stephanie Vial's *The Art of Musical Phrasing* for an in-depth exploration of the relationship between musical articulation and speech.
3. See the Appendix for a graphical comparison of the overtone structures of a Steinway and a Walter piano.
4. L. Mozart, *Treatise*, xxiv.
5. C. P. E. Bach, *Essay*, 155.
6. Türk, *Klavierschule*, 345.
7. Türk, *Klavierschule*, 342.
8. Adam, *Méthode*, 154.
9. Pollini, *Metodo*, 59.
10. L. Mozart, *Treatise*, 218.
11. Cramer, *Magazin*, 1217. Cramer's remarks about Bach appear as a footnote to a report from England by Robert Bremner. Bremner rails against the use of vibrato in instrumental music; Cramer defends its use by praising the expressive power of Bach's playing, which included *Bebung* (vibrato) as well as the dynamic shading alluded to here.
12. Türk, *Klavierschule*, 324.
13. L. Mozart, *Treatise*, 219.
14. Quantz, *Flute*, 254.
15. L. Mozart, *Treatise*, 219.
16. Quantz, *Flute*, 123.
17. L. Mozart, *Treatise*, 41.
18. Türk, *Klavierschule*, 350.
19. Eigeldinger, *Chopin*, 56.
20. There is a growing literature on music and rhetoric, e.g., Beghin and Goldberg, *Haydn and the Performance of Rhetoric*; Tarling, *Weapons of Rhetoric*.
21. "[In *tremolando*] the release and retaking of the pedal must happen so quickly so as to leave no dry gaps." Czerny, *Vollständige theoretisch-practische Pianoforte-Schule*, vol. 3, p. 45. And also: "A quick release and retaking of the pedal must be so well practiced that one scarcely notices it." Czerny, *Vollständige theoretisch-practische Pianoforte-Schule*, vol. 3, p. 46. Yet his examples still show the pedal going *down* with the bass notes, with the release during the previous beat.
22. Türk, *Klavierschule*, 343.

Chapter Three

1. C. P. E. Bach, *Essay*, 36.
2. C. P. E. Bach, *Essay*, 37.

3. Libin, "Emergence," 25–27.
4. Maria Anna Mozart to L. Mozart, December 28, 1777, in Anderson, *Letters of Mozart*, vol. 2, 644.
5. Deutsch, *Mozart*, 153.
6. Haydn to Marianne von Genzinger, July 4, 1790, in Landon, *Correspondence*, 107.
7. Larsen et al., *Haydn Studies*. Panelists were William Newman, Christa Landon, H. C. Robbins Landon, and Jens Peter Larsen.
8. Somfai, *Haydn*, 23.
9. Pollack, *Thoughts*, 76.
10. Burney, *The Present State*, 278–9.
11. Johann Friedrich von Schönfeld, *Jahrbuch der Tonkunst*, 1796, quoted and translated in Skowroneck, *Beethoven*, 76.
12. W. A. Mozart to L. Mozart, October 17, 1777, in Anderson, *Letters of Mozart*, vol. 2, 479.
13. L. Mozart to Maria Anna Mozart, March 12, 1785, in Anderson, *Letters of Mozart*, vol. 3, 1325.
14. W. A. Mozart to L. Mozart, February 28, 1778, in Anderson, *Letters of Mozart*, vol. 2, 736.
15. Some five-octave pianos from the period actually had sixty-three notes, with the upper range extended to g^3. Mozart's own piano only reached f^3; he wrote beyond that range only in one of the parts of the Sonata for Two Pianos, K. 448. Presumably his student Josephine von Aurnhammer, with whom he performed that piece, had a piano with the additional notes. Today, most builders of five-octave fortepianos include them too.
16. Maria Rose argues that this unusually thick accompaniment reflects Mozart's response to the English-style square pianos popular in Paris, where the sonata was composed. See Rose, "Mozart in Paris."
17. Whether the stroke is an independent sign, or simply a large dot, is discussed on p. 12.
18. L. Mozart, *Treatise*, 123–24.
19. C. P. E. Bach, *Essay*, 154.
20. Badura-Skoda, *Interpreting Mozart* (1962), 53.
21. Artaria's edition of this sonata has two one-measure slurs here. But two-measure slurs appear elsewhere in the same publication, e.g., in the third movement of K. 330.
22. Badura-Skoda, *Interpreting Mozart* (1962), 56.
23. Surprisingly, the English words the Badura-Skodas give to the opening of K. 332, *Come and play and sing with pleasure!*, suggest an entirely different interpretation from the Italian ones. Certainly no one would put a comma after the instances of "and" in this sentence, which would correspond to the Italian text (*Canta, canta = Come and, play and, . . .*). The natural division of these

words—*Come* | *and play* | *and sing*—would lead a player to treat each quarter note as an upbeat to the following measure, exactly the reverse of Mozart's grouping. Both the English text and the upbeat-oriented rendition emphasize the continuity of the line, and minimize the smaller articulations, just as Lebert's edition does. No interruptions of the airflow in this version!

24. Badura-Skoda, *Interpreting Mozart* (2008), 119.

25. "according to a communication from Czerny to Otto Jahn, Beethoven had explained to him that he had heard Mozart play: 'had a fine but choppy (*zerhacktes*) way of playing, no *ligato*.'" Thayer, *Beethoven*, 88.

26. Türk, *Klavierschule*, 330.

27. Marpurg, *Anleitung*, 29.

28. C. P. E. Bach, *Essay*, 149

29. A two-manual harpsichord allows for a contrast between *forte* and *piano*, as J. S. Bach specifies in the *Italian Concerto*, the *French Overture*, and several of the *Goldberg Variations*, his only keyboard works that specify such an instrument. But many harpsichords had a single keyboard, with a fixed registration.

30. Cited in Libin, "Emergence," 2.

31. Mozart's Walter seems to have been built with a hand-operated damper control; the knee lever was apparently a later modification (perhaps at Mozart's request when he acquired the instrument). See Latcham, "Mozart and the pianos of Gabriel Anton Walter."

32. I alluded to this technique in connection with K. 332 (see p. 40); the same applies to the opening of K. 283 and other similar accompaniments.

33. Letter dated October 17, 1777.

34. C. P. E. Bach, *Essay*, 431.

35. Leon Fleisher (1958), Christoph Eschenbach (1971), Claudio Arrau (1987), at $\downarrow$ = 28–32!

36. Rosenblum, *Performance Practices*, 63.

37. Chopin's "nocturne style" is a further development of this technique, where the addition of pedal allows the left hand to range over a span of two octaves or more.

38. We certainly should, since much excellent music has been conveniently collected in the 20-volume set *The London Pianoforte School*, edited by Nicholas Temperley.

39. "Haydn . . . told Salomon that he should stay the summer in England, and that as he heard there were to be twelve concerts and two benefits during the season there would be ample time for him to compose his first symphonies after he had the opportunity of studying the taste of the English." From vol. 2, p. 290, of C. Papendiek, *Court and Private Life in the Time of Queen Charlotte: being the Journals of Mrs. Papendiek, Assistant Keeper of the Wardrobe and Reader to Her Majesty* (London 1886), quoted in Landon, *Chronicle*, vol. 4, 509.

40. Mozart commented on Clementi's use of thirds in a letter to his father from January 12, 1782: "Clementi plays well, as far as execution with the right-hand goes. His greatest strength lies in his passages in 3rds. Apart from that, he has not a kreuzer's worth of taste or feeling—in short, he is a mere *mechanicus*." In Anderson, *Letters of Mozart*, vol. 3, 1179.

41. The slur shown in parentheses in measure 4 appears in the first Viennese edition, but not in Haydn's autograph or the original English edition. This could have been a simple oversight, or it may have been part of Haydn's original plan.

42. The third one, Hob. XVI:51 in D major, is an oddity: a relatively easy two-movement work that takes scarcely six minutes to play.

43. Tom Beghin, in his *Virtual Haydn* recording project (Naxos 8.501203), performs the E-flat sonata twice: once on an English instrument (reading from the English edition) and again on a Viennese instrument (reading from the Viennese edition). The English edition follows the autograph; Beghin feels that small discrepancies in the Artaria (Viennese) version may reflect adjustments made to accommodate the Viennese instrument and performance style. (See Beghin, *The Virtual Haydn*, 231–35.)

Chapter Four

1. Czerny, *Proper Performance*, 6.

2. Beethoven to J. A. Streicher, November 19, 1796, in Anderson, *Letters of Beethoven*, vol. 1, 24.

3. "When I feel out of sorts, I play on an Erard piano where I easily find a ready-made tone. But when I feel in good form and strong enough to find my own individual sound, then I need a Pleyel piano." Quoted in Eigeldinger, *Chopin*, 26.

4. Beethoven's instrument had little in common with the Erards Chopin played in Paris in the 1830s, apart from the name on the fallboard.

5. Quoted in Skowroneck, *Beethoven*, 97.

6. Skowroneck, *Beethoven*, 91–92.

7. Skowroneck, *Beethoven*, 57.

8. Czerny, *Proper Performance*, 4.

9. See Rose, "Beethoven and his French Piano."

10. A database of early pianos listing dates and compass can be found at db.earlypiano.org. A search for instruments made in Vienna showed that, while there were a few pianos with c^4 as early as 1802 (including some by Streicher), many were still being made that stopped at g^3 or a^3.

11. Letter to Streicher, quoted in Skowroneck, *Beethoven*, 88.

12. Liszt acquired it after Beethoven's death; his estate donated it to the Hungarian National Museum in Budapest in 1886, where it has remained to this day. It

was restored to playing condition in 1997, when Melvyn Tan used it for a tour and recording.

13. Taub, *Playing Beethoven*, 16

14. Claves CD 9707-10, a complete recording of the Beethoven sonatas on period instruments, presents the early sonatas on earlier pianos, later sonatas on later pianos.

15. Taub, *Playing Beethoven*, 92.

16. Rosen, *Beethoven*, xi.

17. Rosen, *The Romantic Generation*, 1–3.

18. See Rosenblum, *Performance Practices*, 328–29, for a discussion of this problem.

19. I'm not suggesting that Czerny has the last word on Beethoven: even when simply quoting Beethoven's texts, he is not always reliable (see the discussion of op. 26 on pp. 87–88). Czerny's motives are questioned by James Parakilas (see Parakilas, "Playing Beethoven His Way").

20. Rosenblum, *Performance Practices*, 355–61.

21. Perhaps this explains the *Hammerklavier* sonata problem: $\lrcorner$ = 138 is perfectly suitable for the first four bars . . .

22. Schindler, *Biography*, quoted in Barth, *The Pianist as Orator*, 66–67.

23. Wegeler and Ries, *Beethoven Remembered*, 94.

24. Czerny, *Proper Performance*, 33, 35, 36.

25. Philip, *Early Recordings and Musical Style*.

26. Quoted in Skowroneck, *Beethoven*, 146–47.

27. See Rosenblum, *Performance Practices*, 151–52.

28. Czerny, *Proper Performance*, 5.

29. Kalkbrenner, *Anweisung*, 14.

30. Some editors used this argument to justify the replacement of shorter slurs with long ones. As we have seen, even the Badura-Skodas refer to the "established practice" of treating a series of bar-long slurs as continuous legato.

31. Beethoven to Karl Holz, August 15, 1825, in Anderson, *Letters of Beethoven*, vol. 3, 1241.

32. Newman, *Beethoven on Beethoven*, 129–30.

33. Rosen, *Beethoven*, 39.

34. Barth, *The Pianist as Orator*, 88–89.

35. "He used a lot of pedal, much more than is indicated in his works." Czerny, *Proper Performance*, 16.

36. Banowetz, *Pianist's Guide*, 13.

37. This is the core argument of my DMA dissertation: Breitman, "The Damper Pedal and the Beethoven Piano Sonatas."

38. Milchmeyer, *Die wahre Art*, 58.

39. A strip of cloth or leather that, when pressed against the strings, reduced their vibrations, was known variously as a harp-, lute-, or buff stop.

40. Some pianos had a system of shutters that allowed sound to emerge through the lid; others had a pedal that actually raised the entire lid.

41. *Allgemeine Musikalische Zeitung* 1 (1798–99), p. 136. Quoted in Rowland, *A History*, 40.

42. Czerny, "Recollections," 309.

43. Hummel, *A Complete Theoretical and Practical Course*, vol. 3, p. 62. The second example also prescribes the use of the "Pianozug" (soft pedal); his placement of the triangle symbols appears to suggest taking the soft pedal only after the initial chords of mm. 1–3 have sounded.

44. "*Senza ped*"—a totally unambiguous way of specifying where not to use the pedal—was indicated only twice by Beethoven, in two chamber works from around 1801: in variation 5 of the Violin Sonata op. 31, no. 1, mvt. 3, and at the end of the cello variations WoO 46.

45. Beethoven's instructions, as printed in the first edition of op. 27, no. 2 (Cappi, 1801).

46. In my experience it depends on the particular fortepiano and on the acoustics of the room. It helps to use the moderator (if there is one); perhaps the "harp stop" praised by Milchmeyer would be even more effective here.

47. Czerny, *Proper Performance*, 49.

48. Czerny, "Recollections," 309.

49. Czerny, *Proper Performance*, 53.

50. Banowetz, *Pianist's Guide*, 167–78.

51. The penultimate bar of the second example looks like syncopated pedaling—or perhaps there is simply a missing release sign. Scans of several copies of this book can be seen on imslp, and the pedal indications in these bars are inconsistent: one version kept the pedal down while the bass moves chromatically C–C♯–D, with another pedal at the E, and no release sign at all.

52. Czerny, *Vollständige theoretisch-practische Pianoforte-Schule*, vol. 3, p. 43.

53. Here is the original German text: Allein um diese Wirkung hervorzubringen, muss der Spieler das *Pedal* genau mit der *Octave* z u g l e i c h andrücken; denn auch nur um einen Augenblick später, wirkt das *Pedal* nicht mehr, und die *Octave* bleibt kurz und trocken. Da ferner diese *Octave* durch den ganzen Takt klingen soll, so darf er das *Pedal* nicht eher auslassen, als mit der letzten Achtel, um es dann mit der nächsten *Octave* sogleich wieder zu nehmen.

54. Skowroneck, *Beethoven*, 214–15.

55. The Parisian pianist Friedrich Kalkbrenner (1785–1849) used this technique in 1824 to modify a Viennese piano that he found too dry. (Kalkbrenner, *Anweisung*, 10, quoted in Skowroneck, *Beethoven*, 162–63.)

56. Beethoven's letter was quoted and discussed on p. 80 .

57. A literal application of the diminuendo rule works well for slurs covering two or three notes. But as the slurs get longer, more influence is exerted by other factors (high notes, long notes, dissonances)—as in this example.

Chapter Five

1. Andreas Staier and Alexei Lubimov recorded the piece on a Graf replica with the janissary stop: Teldec #0630171132. The full effect can be heard starting at the five-minute mark. On YouTube at the time of writing, at https://www. youtube.com/watch?v=gdKLKomw74k.
2. Schiff, *Schubert*, liner notes.
3. De Silva, *Fortepiano Writings*, 249.
4. Andreas Streicher, "*Brief manual on the proper use and knowledge concerning the playing, tuning, and maintenance of fortepianos*," in De Silva, 53.
5. De Silva, 259.

Chapter Six

1. Eigeldinger, *Chopin*, 91–92.
2. Some of these were in handwritten annotations by Chopin in his pupils' scores; others reflect differences among the multiple first editions (Chopin typically dealt with English, French, and German publishers). High-resolution images of these editions can be found online at www.chopinonline.ac.uk/cfeo (Chopin First Editions Online).
3. Sand, *Autobiography*, 1108.
4. Dated October 19, 2017. Accessed October 13, 2019 at https://en.chopin. nifc.pl/institute/events/news/id/4323. The entire competition can be viewed on the Institute's website: http://iccpi.eu/en/iccpi/multimedia_videos.
5. Eigeldinger, *Chopin*, p. 56: "His specialty was extreme delicacy, and his *pianissimo* extraordinary"; "Chopin played generally very quietly, and rarely, indeed hardly ever, *fortissimo*."
6. Eigeldinger, *Chopin*, 5.
7. Quoted in Eigeldinger, *Chopin*, 49.
8. Eigeldinger, *Chopin*, 50.
9. Hudson, *Stolen Time*, 1.
10. Quantz, *On Playing the Flute*, 252–53.
11. C. P. E. Bach, *Essay*, 161.
12. W. A. Mozart to L. Mozart, October 24, 1777, in Anderson, *Letters of Mozart*, vol. 2, 497.
13. Saint-Saëns, "Quelques mots," 387. He claims to have this on the authority of the singer, pianist, and composer Pauline Viardot, who knew Chopin well.
14. Eigeldinger, *Chopin*, 77–78.
15. Saint-Saëns, "Quelques mots," 387.

16. They are present in the autographs and first editions (although these sources don't always agree), and, for the most part, have been reproduced accurately in later editions.

17. Eigeldinger's *Chopin* has a collection of quotes (on pp. 57–58) which reinforce the importance of the pedals for Chopin, including "In the use of the pedal he had likewise attained the greatest mastery, was uncommonly strict regarding the misuse of it, and said repeatedly to the pupil: 'The correct employment of it remains a study for life'"; "Use the pedal with the greatest economy"; "Chopin used the pedals with the greatest discretion"; "Chopin brought [use of the pedals] to perfection."

18. Chopin's strategy here is the mirror image of my interpretation of the Scherzo from Beethoven's op. 2, no. 3; see p. 116.

19. The precise moment for releasing the pedal is unclear. The autograph shows the release sign midway between the fifth and sixth eighths; the English and French editions place it under the fifth, while the German edition puts it under the last eighth of the bar. All the sources agree, however, that the first half of the second measure is unpedaled.

20. Peru, in Eigeldinger, *Chopin*, 56.

21. Marmontel, in Eigeldinger, *Chopin*, 58.

22. Kleczynski, in Eigeldinger, *Chopin*, 58.

23. Regarding terminology: the damper pedal was called the *loud* or *forte* pedal very early on, but even the earliest writers commented that the term was misleading, since the *forte* pedal was of great use in *piano* passages. In writing about the pedal, authors have traditionally complained that players misuse the pedals, with the damper pedal depressed in all loud passages, and the soft pedal correspondingly overused in soft passages.

24. Robert Philip, Timothy Day, and Neal Peres da Costa have listened very carefully and written insightfully about this material.

Chapter Seven

1. "Griepenkerl, quoted in Speerstra, *J. S. Bach and the Pedal Clavichord*, 170.

2. "The inequality of the fingers as regards strength and flexibility however makes yet another artistic resource necessary . . . J. S. Bach found this resource in the use of the weight of the hand and arm . . ." Griepenkerl, quoted in Speerstra, *J. S. Bach and the Pedal Clavichord*, 167.

3. Extracted from Table 6.1 in Speerstra, *J. S. Bach and the Pedal Clavichord*, 121–23.

4. Separate and articulate, but not uniform. Downbows were for the "good notes" (strong beats or parts of beats); upbows for the "bad" (weak) notes. Similarly,

flute tonguings used paired syllables (tu–ru) to produce an inflected series of notes.

5. I use "deeply" here in its most literal sense. The longer strings are more flexible, and the tangent can raise them further. On each of my clavichords, the key travel for CC is roughly *double* that of c³.

Epilogue

1. Stravinsky, *Poetics*, 129.
2. Spohr, *Violinschule*, 181–82.
3. Stravinsky, *Poetics*, 131.
4. Levinson and Balkin, "Law, Music, and Other Performing Arts," 1627.
5. Levinson and Balkin, "Law, Music, and Other Performing Arts," 1630.
6. Levinson and Balkin, "Law, Music, and Other Performing Arts," 1655, quoting R. Waterston on architecture.
7. Republished in Taruskin, *Text and Act*, 90–104.
8. Crutchfield, "Fashion, Conviction, and Performance Style in an Age of Revivals."
9. Levinson and Balkin, "Law, Music, and Other Performing Arts," 1632.
10. Türk, *Klavierschule*, 321.
11. Türk, *Klavierschule*, 322.
12. C. P. E. Bach, *Essay*, 147–48.
13. Stravinsky, *Poetics*, 68.
14. Stravinsky, *Poetics*, 27.

Bibliography

Adam, Louis. *Méthode de Piano.* Paris: Louis, Marchand de Musique, 1804.

Anderson, Emily, ed. and trans. *The Letters of Beethoven.* London: Macmillan, 1961.

———. *The Letters of Mozart and his Family.* New York: Norton, 1985.

Bach, Carl Philipp Emanuel. *Essay on the True Art of Playing Keyboard Instruments.* Translated by Wm. Mitchell. New York: Norton, 1948.

———. *Probestücke, Leichte and Damen Sonatas.* Edited by David Schulenberg. Los Altos, CA: Packard Humanities Institute, 2005.

Bach, Johann Sebastian. *Inventionen und Sinfonien.* Edited by Georg von Dadelsen. Kassel: Bärenreiter, 1970/2002.

Badura-Skoda, Eva and Paul. *Interpreting Mozart on the Keyboard.* Translated by Leo Black. London: Barrie & Radcliffe, 1962.

———. *Interpreting Mozart: The Performance of His Piano Pieces and Other Compositions.* 2nd ed. New York: Routledge, 2008.

Banowetz, Joseph. *The Pianist's Guide to Pedaling.* Bloomington, IN: Indiana University Press, 1985.

Barth, George. *The Pianist as Orator.* Ithaca, NY: Cornell University Press, 1992.

Beethoven, Ludwig van. *Klaviersonaten.* Edited by Bertha Wallner. Munich: Henle, 1952/1980.

———. *The 35 Piano Sonatas.* Edited by Barry Cooper. London: Associated Board of the Royal Schools of Music, 2007.

———. *32 Sonatas for the Pianoforte.* Edited by Artur Schnabel. New York: Simon & Schuster, 1935.

———. *The 32 Sonatas in Reprints of the First and Early Editions.* London: Tecla Editions, 1989.

Beghin, Tom. *The Virtual Haydn.* Chicago: University of Chicago Press, 2015.

Beghin, Tom and Sander M. Goldberg, eds., *Haydn and the Performance of Rhetoric.* Chicago: University of Chicago Press, 2007.

Bilson, Malcolm. *Knowing the Score.* DVD. Cornell University, 2005.

———. *Performing the Score.* DVD. Cornell University, 2011.

Breitman, David. "The Damper Pedal and the Beethoven Piano Sonatas: A Historical Perspective." DMA diss., Cornell University, 1994.

Brown, A. Peter. *Joseph Haydn's Keyboard Music: Sources and Style.* Bloomington, IN: University of Indiana Press, 1986.

Brown, Clive. *Classical and Romantic Performing Practice: 1750–1900*. New York: Oxford University Press, 1999.

Burney, Charles. *The Present State of Music in Germany, The Netherlands and United Provinces*. London: Becket, Robson, and Robinson, 1773.

Cramer, Carl Friedrich. *Magazin der Music*. Hamburg: Musicalischen Niederlage, 1783.

Crutchfield, Will. "Fashion, Conviction, and Performance Style in an Age of Revivals." In *Authenticity and Early Music*, edited by Nicholas Kenyon, 19–26. New York: Oxford University Press, 1988.

Czerny, Carl. *On the Proper Performance of All Beethoven's Works for the Piano [Über den richtigen Vortrag der sämtlichen Beethoven'schen Klavierwerke]*. Originally Part IV of *Vollständige theoretisch-practische Pianoforte-Schule*. Vienna, 1842. English trans. London: 1846. Facsimile editions edited by Paul Badura-Skoda. Vienna: Universal, 1963 (German); 1970 (English).

———. "Recollections from My Life." *Musical Quarterly* 42 (1956): 302–17.

———. *Vollständige theoretisch-practische Pianoforte-Schule* [Complete Theoretical-practical Pianoforte Method], op. 500. Vienna: Diabelli, 1842.

Day, Timothy. *A Century of Recorded Music*. New Haven, CT: Yale University Press, 2002.

De Silva, Preethi. *Fortepiano Writings of Streicher, Dieudonné, and the Schiedmayers*. Lewiston, NY: Edwards Mellen Press, 2009.

Deutsch, Otto. *Mozart: A Documentary Biography*. Stanford, CA: Stanford University Press, 1965.

Eigeldinger, Jean-Jacques. *Chopin: Pianist and Teacher*. Cambridge: Cambridge University Press, 1989.

Everett-Green, Robert. "Does he have the right stuff?" [interview with Pinchas Zukerman] *Toronto Globe and Mail*, March 8, 2000. Accessed May 7, 2018. https://www.theglobeandmail.com/arts/does-he-have-the-right-stuff/article18421452/.

Gunn, Donna Louise. *Discoveries from the Fortepiano*. New York: Oxford University Press, 2016.

Harnoncourt, Nikolaus. *Baroque Music Today*. Portland, OR: Amadeus Press, 1995.

Haynes, Bruce. *The End of Early Music*. New York: Oxford University Press, 2007.

Hudson, Richard. *Stolen Time: The History of Tempo Rubato*. New York: Oxford University Press, 1994.

Hummel, Johann Nepomuk. *Ausführliche theoretisch-practische Anweisung*. Vienna: Haslinger, 1827.

———. *A Complete Theoretical and Practical Course of Instructions on the Art of Playing the Piano Forte, Commencing with the Simplest Elementary Principles and Including Every Information Requisite to the Most Finished Style of Performance*. London: Boosey, 1828.

Kalkbrenner, Friedrich. *Anweisung das Pianoforte mit Hülfe des Handleiters spielen zu lernen*. Leipzig: Fr. Kistner, 1832.

Kenyon, Nicholas, ed. *Authenticity and Early Music.* New York: Oxford University Press, 1988.

Komlos, Katalin. *Fortepianos and their Music.* New York: Oxford University Press, 1995.

Landon, H. C. Robbins. *The Collected Correspondence and London Notebooks of Joseph Haydn.* London: Barrie and Rockliff, 1959.

———. *Haydn: Chronicle and Works.* Bloomington, IN: Indiana University Press, 1976–80.

Larsen, Jens Peter, Howard Serwer, and James Webster, eds. *Haydn Studies: Proceedings of the International Haydn Conference.* New York: Norton, 1981.

Latcham, Michael. "Mozart and the Pianos of Gabriel Anton Walter." *Early Music* 25, no. 3 (1997): 382–400.

Levinson, Sanford and J. M. Balkin. "Law, Music, and Other Performing Arts." *University of Pennsylvania Law Review* 139, no. 6 (1991): 1597–658. Accessed May 7, 2018. http://scholarship.law.upenn.edu/penn_law_review/vol139/iss6/4.

Libin, Kathryn L. Shanks. "The Emergence of an Idiomatic Fortepiano Style in the Keyboard Concertos of Mozart." PhD diss., New York University, 1998.

Marpurg, Friedrich Wilhelm. *Anleitung zum Klavierspielen.* 1755. Facsimile of the first edition. New York: Broude, 1969.

Milchmeyer, Johann Peter. *Die wahre Art das Pianoforte zu spiele.* Dresden: Carl Christian Meinhold, 1797.

Mozart, Leopold. *A Treatise on the Fundamentals of Violin Playing.* Translated by E. Knocker. New York: Oxford University Press, 1985.

Mozart, Wolfgang Amadeus. *NMA Online = Neue Mozart Ausgabe: Digitized Version.* Salzburg: Internationale Stiftung Mozarteum, n.d.

———. *19 Sonatas for the Piano.* Edited by Richard Epstein. New York: G. Schirmer, 1893.

———. *Sonatas for Piano.* Edited by Sigmund Lebert. New York: Carl Fischer, n.d.

Newman, William. *Beethoven on Beethoven.* New York: Norton, 1991.

Oort, Bart van. "The English Classical Piano Style and its influence on Haydn and Beethoven." DMA diss., Cornell University, 1993.

Parakilas, James. "Playing Beethoven His Way: Czerny and the Canonization of Performance Practice." In *Beyond The Art of Finger Dexterity: Reassessing Carl Czerny,* edited by David Gramit. Rochester, NY: University of Rochester Press, 2008.

———, ed. *Piano Roles.* New Haven, CT: Yale University Press, 1999.

Pay, Anthony. "Phrasing in Contention." *Early Music* 24, no. 2 (1996): 291–321.

Peres da Costa, Neal. *Off the Record.* New York: Oxford University Press, 2012.

Philip, Robert. *Early Recordings and Musical Style: Changing Tastes in Instrumental Performance, 1900–1950.* Cambridge: Cambridge University Press, 1992.

Pollack, Howard. "Some Thoughts on the 'Clavier' in Haydn's Solo Claviersonaten." *The Journal of Musicology* 9, no. 1 (1991): 74–91.

Pollini, Francesco. *Metodo per Clavicembalo.* Milan: G. Ricordi, 1811.

Quantz, Johann Joachim. *Versuch einer Anweisung die Flöte traversiere zu spielen.* Translated by Edward R. Reilly as *On Playing the Flute.* Boston: Northeastern University Press, 2001.

Rose, Maria. "Beethoven and his French Piano: Proof of Purchase." *Musique, Images, Instruments* 7 (2005): 110–22.

———. "Mozart in Paris: Which Piano is Appropriate for Sonata K. 310?" *Early Keyboard Journal* 24 (2006): 7–37.

Rosen, Charles. *Beethoven's Piano Sonatas: A Short Companion.* New Haven, CT: Yale University Press, 2002.

———. *The Romantic Generation.* Cambridge, MA: Harvard University Press, 1995.

Rosenblum, Sandra. *Performance Practices in Classic Piano Music.* Bloomington, IN: Indiana University Press, 1988.

Rowland, David. *A History of Pianoforte Pedaling.* Cambridge: Cambridge University Press, 1993.

Saint-Saëns, Camille. "Quelques mots sur l'exécution des oeuvres de Chopin." *Le courrier musical* 13, no. 1 (1910): 386–87.

Sand, George. *Story of My Life: The Autobiography of George Sand.* Edited by Thelma Jurgrau. Albany, NY: State University Press of New York, 1991.

Schiff, András. "Confessions of a Convert: Schubert on the Fortepiano." Essay included in the liner notes to the CD recording *Franz Schubert: Impromptus, Sonatas, & Moments Musicaux,* ECM 2425/26, 2015.

Skowroneck, Tilman. *Beethoven the Pianist.* Cambridge: Cambridge University Press, 2010.

Somfai, Laszlo. *The Keyboard Sonatas of Joseph Haydn.* Translated by Charlotte Greenspan. Chicago: University of Chicago Press, 1995.

Speerstra, Joel. *J. S. Bach and the Pedal Clavichord: An Organist's Guide.* Rochester, NY: University of Rochester Press, 2004.

Spohr, Louis. *Violinschule.* 1832. Translated by John Bishop as *Louis Spohr's Celebrated Violin School.* London: R. Cocks, 1843.

Stravinsky, Igor. *Poetics of Music in the Form of Six Lessons.* Cambridge, MA: Harvard University Press, 1947.

Tarling, Judy. *The Weapons of Rhetoric: A Guide for Musicians and Audiences.* St. Albans, Hertfordshire: Corda Music, 2004.

Taruskin, Richard. *Text and Act.* New York: Oxford University Press, 1995.

Taub, Robert. *Playing the Beethoven Piano Sonatas.* Portland, OR: Amadeus, 2003.

Temperley, Nicholas, ed. *The London Pianoforte School.* New York: Garland, 1984–87.

Thayer, Alexander Wheelock. *Thayer's Life of Beethoven.* Princeton, NJ: Princeton University Press, 1991.

Türk, Daniel Gottlob. *Klavierschule.* 1789. Translated by Raymond H. Haggh as *School of Clavier Playing.* Lincoln, NE: University of Nebraska Press, 1982.

Vial, Stephanie. *The Art of Musical Phrasing in the Eighteenth Century: Punctuating the Classical "Period."* Rochester, NY: University of Rochester Press, 2008.

Walden, Daniel K. S. "PianoFortePiano: Exploring the Use of Historical Keyboards as a Heuristic Guide to Performance on the Modern Piano." *MTNA e-Journal* (November 2010): 12–21.

Wegeler, Franz Gerhard, and Ferdinand Ries. *Beethoven Remembered: The Biographical Notes of Franz Wegeler and Ferdinand Ries.* Arlington, VA: Great Ocean Publishers, 1987.

Index of Works

General Index

www.ingramcontent.com/pod-product-compliance
Lightning Source LLC
Chambersburg PA
CBHW071008140426
42814CB00004BA/166